HST
The Train that Saved Britain's Railways

Andrew Royle

crecy.co.uk

First published in 2021 by Crécy Publishing

All rights reserved. No part of this book may be reproduced or transmitted in any form or by any means electronic or mechanical, including photocopying, recording or by any information storage without permission from the Publisher in writing. All enquiries should be directed to the Publisher.

© Text Andrew Royle 2021

A CIP record for this book is available from the British Library

Printed in Bulgaria by Multiprint

ISBN 978 1 91080 998 3

Crécy Publishing Limited
1a Ringway Trading Estate, Shadowmoss Road, Manchester M22 5LH
www.crecy.co.uk

FRONT COVER On 15 September 2012, the 16.15 from St Pancras International to Nottingham hammers up the last few yards of Sharnbrook Bank behind 43060. The Paxman VP185 engine fitted to this and other power cars used on the MML may have lacked the scream of the Valenta's turbocharger but it made its own impression nevertheless.

BACK COVER MAIN At the top of the Rockstone footbridge on 25 September 2020, early evening sunshine illuminates the track beautifully for about half an hour or so before the shadows creep in too much. No. 43093 *Old Oak Common HST Depot 1976-2018* heads 2C34 16.22 Exeter St David's–Penzance; the inset sliding doors on the coaches of these sets can be discerned.

INSET CLOCKWISE FROM TOP On Christmas Day 1989, our keen photographer has taken advantage of the annual network shutdown to obtain this view of HSTs taking a rare moment to rest at St Philip's Marsh depot. No. 43003 is the nearest power car. *Arthur Turner/Transport Treasury*

Blackford is on the main line between Perth and Stirling, where we find 43274 *Spirit of Sunderland* heading the diverted 09.10 Edinburgh to Aberdeen (with 43313 the trailing power car) on 14 February 2016. *Ian Lothian*

Ferrybridge C Power Station provides the backdrop to this power car move for 43185 *Great Western* in InterCity 'Swallow' livery and 43002 *Sir Kenneth Grange* in original livery. *Jason Rogers*

On 13 September 2018, 43190 is digging into the climb of Rattery Bank, which faces all westbound trains from the moment they leave Totnes station.

FRONTISPIECE Record breaking power car 43102 flashes across the River Ouse at Radwell on 28 February 2021, a cloudless and sunny Sunday afternoon. The previous week it had been named 'The Journey Shrinker', harking back to one of British Rail's clever marketing catchlines but also marking the end of HST operations over the Midland route to London.

Contents

Introduction 4

BR Rings the Changes 5

Go West 18

On Location 42

Motive Power Matters 64

The Human Element 94

Colourful HSTs 108

Look North 132

In the Picture 148

Out of the Ordinary 172

Ever Onward… 186

Bibliography 188

Index 189

Introduction

It's July 1982, the train drivers are on strike and the railways are at a standstill. On the desk of the Transport Minister sits an outline for the coming Serpell Report, a set of proposals that could slash the nation's rail system to a shadow of what even Beeching envisaged. Prime Minister Margaret Thatcher has spoken of the 'great car economy' and soon she will open a completed M25 orbital motorway that will speed traffic around the capital, supposedly relieving London of many traffic jams. Things could hardly look much worse for rail's supporters.

But already the last vehicles of the High Speed Train fleet are being delivered to British Rail and its canny chairman, Peter Parker, is probably the most positive and forward-thinking man there's ever been in that post. The investment that BR made in its research and development facilities, at Derby in particular, is about to start paying off. With the HST as the prime weapon in his armoury, Parker knows he can take on the internal airlines and begin to put the motor car in its place – in the station car park!

Now, we may look back and groan at the thought of those 'This is the Age of the Train' TV commercials but when the inevitable jokes had subsided, people began to make day trips on HSTs to places like Bath and Durham when previously they might never have considered using the train. Businessmen discovered that they could travel 200 miles or more to city centre meetings or to site visits and not be faced with the stress of a long drive home afterwards, often in the dark and feeling hungry too. The HST made that quantum leap in speed and comfort that would turn around the fading fortunes of inter-city rail travel. The commuter belt was also pushed out from cities, London especially, and those who had regularly called for railways to be turned into motorways were silenced.

My first taste of using a High Speed Train came in July 1977 during a day trip to London with my father, courtesy of one of those Kellogg's vouchers. On our return journey to Leamington Spa, instead of waiting for the Birmingham New Street service, we first took an HST as far as Reading. This was in coach W42017 of set 253005. Memories are that the train rode more smoothly and quietly at 125mph than our regular class 47-hauled mark 2 coaches did at 90 (thanks to the air suspension of the mark 3 coach); the sensation of the higher speed only registered when looking out of the window. The decor was a tad garish – this *was* the Seventies – and the ambient lighting quite bright. Downsides were that collecting numbers of other trains at that speed was all but impossible and when the brakes were applied for the Reading stop, a harsh burning smell fed through the air conditioning. The latter problem was eventually cured after several different compounds of brake pad were tried. Passengers in second class sometimes also found themselves with a limited view out of the window – seats were no longer arranged in bays to align with all of them.

My last truly close encounter with the HST was as a technician working on board the New Measurement Train from 2003 to 2012. The work that this train does has undoubtedly led to an improvement in the quality of track across the country and I think I can be excused for including several views of it!

The fact that the HST was able to achieve its higher speeds and stop within the existing signalling arrangements is well documented; often forgotten is that, unlike on the Continent, travelling on such a premium train did not import a premium fare: 'Extra speed, extra comfort at no extra cost' ran the advertising slogan. It may well have been regarded by railway enthusiasts as a nameless and soulless replacement for their beloved Westerns, Deltics, Peaks, class 47s and 50s but the final runs of HSTs out of Paddington and King's Cross were to attract almost as much interest as their predecessors.

When people consider the High Speed Train, the phrase that it 'saved Britain's railways' keeps coming up and I believe it is praise that is well deserved.

Please note that this book is a collection of themes, rather than a chronological account of the train's history. I would like to thank Mick Barstow, Dave Coxon, Robin Fell (at the Transport Treasury), Colin Marsden, Kevin Robertson, Ray Stenning, Ray Lewis, Graham Maxtone, Arthur Richards, and Ross Davidson for their valued assistance with the production, together with the photographers who contributed the material to supplement my own. Lastly, a special mention for NMT driver Jim Daniel who appeared on the front of my other Crécy book *Yellow Trains* – the caption failed to mention him!

BR Rings the Changes

The lifetime of the High Speed Train has been one of change. Whether through ownership, operation or appearance, few aspects of use have not been subject to some kind of alteration, hence it doesn't seem inappropriate to begin this book by considering the early livery changes under British Rail. Debate is ongoing about how often trains might benefit from a new livery; some suggest that there is an optimum timescale involved while others may argue that a full internal refurbishment should accompany it. Few would claim that any livery should be left unchanged until withdrawal. While staff morale is often boosted by a new paint scheme, how much benefit may be obtained through extra revenue is harder to prove.

Executive Traction

On their original introduction, the enhanced performance of the HSTs gave rise to a concern that in certain circumstances a junction turn-out might be negotiated too quickly if the driver failed to reduce speed sufficiently for the diverging route. This led to the introduction of a 'flashing yellow' sequence of signals on the approach to certain critical junctions, for example here at Bristol Patchway. Set 253030 (led by W43129) tops the rise out of Patchway Tunnel on 13 February 1984 and will almost certainly be taking the main route towards Parkway on its Swansea–Paddington working. If one of those three feathers on the colour light signal had been lit (for the Bristol or Avonmouth lines), the train would have received flashing signals from the other side of Patchway Tunnel. Illustrated here is an earlier application of the 'Executive' livery with yellow extended beyond the cooler group, the grey band continued from the top of the coaches through the rooftop grills and a hyphenated Inter-City logo. *Arthur Turner/Transport Treasury*

No. 43069 bursts from the north end of Hadley Wood North Tunnel on 1 May 1986 while working the down 'Tees-Tyne Pullman' (with 43043) and two fairly senior-looking gentlemen are on the footplate. A second man was still required for 125mph running at this time. Having left King's Cross ten minutes or so before at 17.30, the many business travellers on board will be settling down with their newspapers and perhaps a menu for dinner; prices ranged from £7.95 to £10.95. An Executive-class return fare from Newcastle was £99. This particular Pullman service had been reintroduced (now as an HST) the previous September and called at Doncaster, York, Darlington and Durham before reaching Newcastle at 20.48. The 'Yorkshire Pullman' from Leeds had been launched in May with a ground-breaking on-train telephone service available on both services! The 'S' on the triangular sign indicated the presence of spring catch points near the tunnel mouth, largely only being of interest to a train moving in the wrong direction on the down slow line.

The front of 43063 moves off from the platform at Wellingborough on 4 September 1986, heading the 15.15 St Pancras–Sheffield (and having 43044 for company). This stretch of railway was said to be the last remaining four-track section of main line in the country to retain semaphore signalling. Sadly, by the time that modernisation with multiple aspect colour lights had been completed in late 1987, the number of tracks had also been reduced drastically to reflect the declining numbers of trains. The grandeur of the line had been reduced somewhat. Years later, four tracks would have to be restored to cater for a reversal of fortunes, albeit with less freight traffic than previously. It was never easy for BR to introduce HSTs to the St Pancras route due to the insufficient number of units approved for construction by the government.

One year later, 43043 hurries the 12.50 Nottingham–St Pancras down the grade from Sharnbrook Summit (located around a mile or so behind the train) on 5 September 1987. Note the ample provision of first-class accommodation in this set that would also see use on the ECML Pullman services. The 'InterCity 125' legend was kept on the power cars but refurbished coaches just proclaimed 'INTERCITY'. No. 43051 brings up the rear and is passing the site of Souldrop signal box that was positioned in-between the high-level fast lines and lower-level slow lines. The latter were built at a later date with gentler gradients and a tunnel across the line's summit for the sake of heavy freight trains; Wymington Tunnel mouth can just be seen above the third coach. Also of note at this location are the four distinct types of fastening in use on each track: The down main has BJB spring bar clips, the up main has SHC spring hoop clips, the down slow has the familiar Pandrol type while the up slow is jointed rails fixed to wooden sleepers with spikes. All have since been replaced here with more modern fixings, not to mention the accompanying overhead wires.

Here we have a track-level view of 43173 pulling away from Cheltenham Spa with the 16.17 to London Paddington on 1 September 1991. Later named *Swansea University*, this power car became the first of its class to be withdrawn from service following its collision with a freight train at Southall in 1997. While rail accidents involving loss of life are dramatic and grab the headlines, it should not detract from the fact that rail travel is the safest form of land transport by a considerable margin. The High Speed Train is widely regarded as having been one of the safest passenger trains in the world, not least when you consider the mixed-traffic railway on which it has operated. Those accidents involving HSTs could hardly be attributed to any shortcomings in design or maintenance – arguably only the one at Southall. Drivers Brian Cooper (in 1999), Stan Martin (in 2004) and Brett McCullough (in 2020) lost their lives while in control of HSTs. The superb safety record of this train is also in no small part due to the professionalism of railway staff.

Follow the Swallow

The unusual station at Yeovil Pen Mill is the setting for 43016 as it eases a diverted service through there from the West Country to Paddington on 18 May 1991. The train is running slowly between platforms 1 and 2 (the latter not in normal use) as it leaves the single line from Yeovil Junction. The 'Swallow' livery was launched in 1987 with the intention of creating something of a clear distinction from the rest of BR, hence the new typeface and replacement of the double arrow. By this time, the InterCity sector of BR was making a profit in its own right and concentrating on promoting an increasingly recognised brand with various initiatives, some ideas coming from other transport sectors or from retail. 'INTERCITY' (all one word) was now on the side of trains and across all advertising as this side of BR strove to adopt the practices of private industry. Who can forget those TV adverts with the penguin on the passenger's paperback book coming to life, as Leon Redbone's soporific tune 'So, Relax' played in the background? It was around this time that the term 'second class' was altered to 'standard class' for ordinary fares; nobody liked to think of themselves as second-class citizens anymore!

RIGHT Power car 43066 demonstrates the trainspotter-friendly format of numbering at Tupton (north of Chesterfield) while forming the 13.28 from Sheffield to London St Pancras on 25 June 1991. This location was once bustling with freight activity relating to the coal industry, as the former sidings to the right of this view fed the Avenue coking plant in the background. This had been producing coke, smokeless fuels and gas since the 1950s but was clearly being run down as the sidings were now overgrown and wagons had long since ceased crossing the flyover into the works. After closure the following year, it was labelled as one of the most polluted former industrial sites in Europe and took around seven years to clean up. Also of interest is the queue of trains on the up goods line – an example of permissive working: 56040 powers a steel train to Cardiff, 56010 is a light engine and 56004 at the back hauls a loaded MGR train.

LEFT The up 'Cornish Riviera' (08.47 Penzance–Paddington) calls at Exeter St David's on a fine 28 April 1993. No. 43192 has that famous name *City of Truro* and is in a lovely clean condition, displaying the Swallow 'INTERCITY' livery to best effect. This clearly shows that the nameplate finish matched that of the Swallow emblem. On the front coach, the diagonal line across the lower half of the passenger door demonstrates where the bodywork has been shaped to allow maximum clearance on curves. Positioning the doors right at the end of the vehicle facilitated a much wider opening and therefore easier boarding for passengers carrying luggage – just one of the touches that made the mark 3 coach so much better than its predecessors.

A low-angle view of a train coming around a curve can often impart an impression of speed. I had several goes at perfecting this shot; it just happened to be an HST with which I achieved the best result, with the top train of the train not coinciding with the overhead supports or the outline of the bridge and the nose staying clear of the lineside equipment cabinets. Other shots of class 90s failed to make the grade! The location is well known to railway enthusiasts – Heamies Bridge, just to the north of Norton Bridge in Staffordshire. No. 43179 *Pride of Laira* is heading northwards into the evening sun, which was nice and bright on 8 June 1994 at 7.10pm.

RIGHT Dropping down into Temple Meads past the Rail Express Systems depot at Bristol Barton Hill in April 1996 comes the much-travelled 43002, on this occasion apparently without at least one of its *Top of the Pops* nameplates. The original cast plates had been removed in 1988 when the Swallow livery was applied, following an overhaul. However, they were to be replaced by the stainless steel variety in 1991. Both headlights and marker lights were deployed by this time to maximise visibility of the train to trackside workers; for them, at 2 miles a minute an HST set went from being an easily missed spot on the horizon to a very real threat in no time at all. The RES facility was being used to stable the stock of the Royal Train as they had assumed the responsibility of operating it; the coach to the left is thought to be the Duke of Edinburgh's saloon No. 2904, converted in 1977 for Royal Train use from No. 12001 in the prototype HST.
Transport Treasury Archive

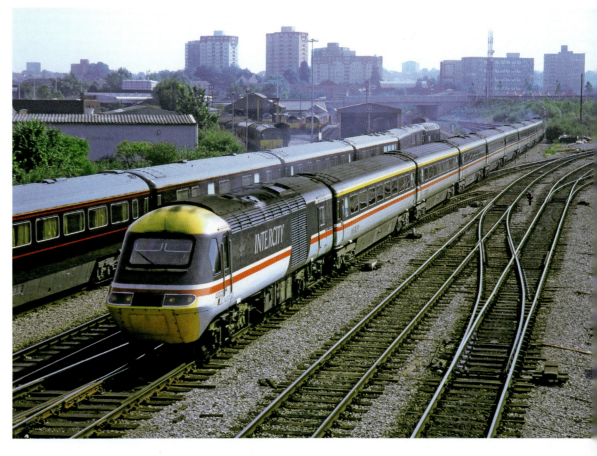

LEFT Initially, it was intended that the first few production power cars would be the ones to receive buffers for trialling DVT operation and 43005 was given an extended yellow frontage (at St Philip's Marsh) in anticipation of this. Other power cars were to be selected instead (43123 being the first) but 43005 still ran in traffic for a time with its bright new face, as seen here leaving Worcester Shrub Hill on 3 September 1988. It is heading a Hereford–Paddington working, supported by 43146. Another feature of this particular repaint was the very small vehicle number applied to the side, just in front of the van door. This was something also to be seen on class 90s and people joked that it was some kind of challenge to the train-spotting fraternity. In practice, it also made life awkward for railway staff! Consequently, larger numbers returned – in the case of HSTs, to below the cab-side window. At the time of this photograph, the author was living in a flat in the block glimpsed to the right of the short signal post in the yard.

Give Me the Works

This is a brand new SC43087, as part of set 254016, prior to delivery to Heaton around May 1978 (but prefixed for allocation to Craigentinny). The actual location is uncertain but believed to be around the Derby Litchurch Lane Works area. ECML HST services had commenced the previous month, though some early members of the 254 fleet had already been borrowed for use on the Western Region. A plan to uprate the Paxman Valenta engines in the East Coast power cars to 2,500hp was abandoned as not being cost effective; basically, the performance benefits were so marginal as not to be worth the extra expense of fuel and maintenance required to obtain them. Note the rain strip fitted below the windscreen to help relieve the workload of the wiper during heavier downpours. *Graham Smith*

Traditionally, diesel locomotives went to railway workshops to receive heavy repairs or full overhauls and this was continued with the HST's class 43 power cars to begin with, Derby Loco Works being the favoured option. However, increasingly the depots to which the trains were allocated were becoming equipped with the means to carry out more and heavier maintenance, until 43188 was the last to be overhauled at Derby in March 1988. During the period leading up to that, 43102 and 43165 receive major attention among the wheelsets and workshop floor detritus on 3 October 1987. No. 43165 appears to be facing its own power unit, while 43102 is possibly closer to being outshopped judging by its glowing lights. *Arthur Turner/Transport Treasury*

LEFT Stratford workshops played host to HST power cars on many occasions and some had buffers fitted there. It's possible there may be a severe problem with the brakes on this four-month old example, E43075, on 11 March 1978, as there is an unusual amount of dirt low down on the vehicle but not so much higher up. 'The Leper Colony' has been scrawled into the grime under the nose and the attached barrier mark 1 coach suggests it has had to be hauled in disgrace from Heaton depot. The growing use of electronics in new rolling stock proved problematical for some employees on the railway, though the intention was that the HST should not become an overly demanding and sophisticated entity that routinely required the attentions of too many maintenance staff. *Arthur Turner/ Transport Treasury*

RIGHT Its career as a prototype and latterly a test vehicle now over, ADB975813 (ex-43001) awaits its fate in the dump area of Derby Loco Works on 3 October 1987. It was to survive another two years before scrapping by Booths at Rotherham in 1990. Although the full prototype set saw a couple of months of further passenger service in 1976, due to delays in delivering the new production sets, the need for drivers to have separate training to 'sign' it meant that it couldn't feasibly become part of the regular fleet in the longer term. *Arthur Turner/ Transport Treasury*

Neville Depot in Leeds was one of those to assume the heavier maintenance role, once Derby Loco Works had closed. On 31 May 2001, 43029 is waiting for attention there as the last power car in the 'Swallow' livery and effectively the final vestige of BR among the fleet. It was to emerge in First Great Western's initial version of the so-called 'Barbie' livery. A Virgin-liveried unit can just be seen to the left of depot shunter 08527 and several heavy spares from 'Railpart' are lying around in shrink-wrap plastic.

Go West

The West of England and South Wales have been associated with the HST since 1976 and continue to be so to this day. From the pleasantly rolling countryside of Wiltshire and Somerset through to the coastal scenery of Devon and Cornwall, there is much of interest to be seen through the carriage window. The writer has always struggled to concentrate for long on any reading matter he may have brought with him on a journey over the former Western Region!

Crofton Curve

Just as the Kennet and Avon Canal did before it, the route of the Berks and Hants line swung through nearly 90 degrees as it sought a way around the Savernake Forest and into the Vale of Pewsey without building too steep a gradient. This took place near the hamlet of Crofton, perhaps better known for the presence of its pumping station and the beam engines installed there to bring water to the summit of the canal. On 28 February 2005, 43028 leads a train for Paddington round the curve, as 43180 brings up the rear. The livery shown was the second attempt at using the bus company First Group's colours on a train with blue, purple and pink and the company logo very prominent. The following year saw the next refurbishment of stock and power cars, bringing another new livery with it. Note the yellow trackside lubricators, so positioned to inhibit the onset of sidewear to the outer rail of each track, while not contaminating the rail head at the same time.

No. 43024 runs onto the top end of the curve on a snowy 8 February 1996 with the 06.35 from Plymouth to Paddington. Noticeable at the front of this power car is the radio antenna, fitted to permit use of the analogue NRN (National Radio Network) by the driver. Although useful to have, this was not the easiest or most effective of systems, as trains would pass from one zone of radio coverage to another and the driver had to remember to manually change channels when prompted by lineside reminder boards. It's also obvious from this how ineffective train headlights used to be. The farmer's bridge here proved too weak and narrow for modern day machinery to cross and has since been removed.

HST – The Train That Saved Britain's Railways

Stepping back from the railway fence to take in a wider view, we have 43187 in 'Merlin' livery working towards London in the early evening of 7 May 1997. The country lane hereabouts offers a convenient stopping point to watch the passage of rail traffic, some of it consisting of the heaviest freight trains in Britain as they transfer quarried limestone from Somerset to Acton Yard, prior to distribution around the London area. There seems to be a quite thundery-looking prospect to the weather in this view and, sure enough, a check of my notes tells me that this was the last photograph I took that day!

A short walk from the previous viewpoint brings us to Crofton lock, adjacent to the pumping station overlooking it. No. 43142 *Reading Panel Signal Box 1965-2010* is just taking the curve at its low end with a down working to the West Country on 8 August 2015. It looks as though Dad is grabbing a photo, while Grandad ensures that their youngest doesn't fall off the lock gate in the excitement. A walk along this canal towpath is a delight in either direction and if you are lucky, you may find that drinks and snacks are on sale from one of those narrowboats. The appeal of watching trains go by in a quiet part of the countryside on a warm sunny day remains undiminished with the passing of time: sixty-plus years before it had been Castles and Kings, forty-odd years ago it was Westerns and class 50s and now we can look back on the reign of the HST with (almost!) equal nostalgia.

Merlin Magic

The newly privatised 'Great Western' franchise sought to combine the emotion of its name with the tried and tested image of the InterCity brand from which it was emerging: Its Merlin symbol seemed to be picking up where the Swallow left off, and very impressive the colour scheme was too. This almost harked back to the livery style of the prototype HST. No. 43183 was one of the power cars at the launch of the new brand at Bristol Temple Meads on 30 September 1995, together with 43185 *Great Western*.

43183 is now seen about to enter Dainton Tunnel from the west on 30 November 1996. The low wall to the left of the track marks the location of Dainton signal box, the so-called 'plywood wonder' version of which stood sentry duty from 1965 to 1987, when it was removed upon resignalling of the area. Some moments after I took this photograph, I witnessed ex-Great Western steam locos 7325 and 6024 *King Edward I* storm towards the tunnel, taking 'The Devonian' rail tour to Worcester.

Clearly showing the Merlin symbol, we have 43008 facing towards London and ready to depart from Bath Spa on a warm summer's evening with the 17.40 Weston super Mare–Paddington on 5 July 1997. 'Express Sprinter' DMU 158839 approaches on the viaduct over the rooftops of this highly picturesque town. It must have been a hot day as you can see the two emergency ventilation hopper windows on each car of the DMU are open; a sure sign that its air conditioning units are struggling, if not completely packed up, as they often did when they were needed the most. In the writer's experience, the air con equipment on the HST's mark 3 coaches was never as unreliable as that on the class 158s.

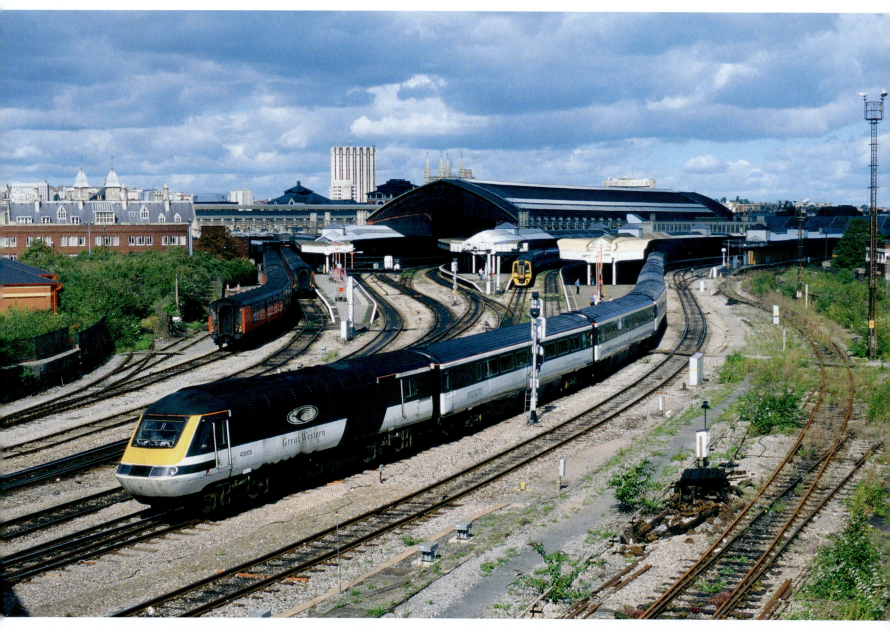

On 13 September 1997, a similar pairing of HST and DMU are found just a few miles away at Bristol Temple Meads. This time it is 43005 leading a set as it draws out of platform 12 on empty coaching stock, presumably to reverse on the carriage line and then run into St Philip's Marsh depot. 'SPM' had by now completely succeeded Bath Road as Bristol's principal depot. The rusty rails and rampant greenery on the right bear testimony to the locomotive depot's fall from grace as (by this date) only a handful of mail and freight trains in the Bristol area required the regular use of locos for motive power. It had closed two years before. Despite this loss of spectator value, it was still reassuring to see a handful of enthusiasts watching proceedings at the country end of this famous station. Note the other patches of greenery in the station's environs: Weed growth on operational tracks, as well as on those out of use, was becoming a concerning feature of the network under Railtrack's administration.

No. 43008 had been transferred from Cross Country to Great Western in the year prior to this photo, so it received the full Merlin treatment. It was only returning to its previous haunts, of course, having been in the first group of trains that were introduced to the Western Region in 1976 as part of set 253004, based at Old Oak Common. It is accelerating away from Worcester Shrub Hill on 2 August 1998 with the 15.45 to Paddington (with 43024 bringing up the rear). On this hot Sunday afternoon, I have staked my spot opposite the Metal Box factory in readiness for 6024 *King Edward I* (again!) to pass almost two hours later with the 'Cotswold Venturer' special. I recall finding this location in plenty of time for the special but feeling very thirsty, not having brought a drink with me. Returning to my car to get one (parked some distance away) would very likely have meant finding another photographer in exclusive residence on my return! The new Great Western franchise saw quiet coaches being introduced to their trains, and a single-manning agreement reached with their drivers led to more 125mph running and some faster schedules as a result.

Ways out West

Spanning this picture at Swindon is the signal gantry from which the well-known photograph of the prototype HST and gas turbine APT alongside each other was taken in August 1975. On 13 March 1994, I could only manage 43026 *City of Westminster* (with 43004 *Swan Hunter*) forming the 10.00 Paddington–Swansea together with another InterCity-liveried set in the far platform 1. You could wait a long time to see any trains using the three tracks on the right; these were the up and down through lines plus the down goods. This had been a legacy from the 1967 decision to demolish the old down platform and remodel the layout to concentrate operations either side of the up island platform, something that would clearly present operational headaches at this busy location. Railway land was released to build a nice new office block (which casts its shadow over part of the train), so that was clearly where priorities lay back then! In 2003, the down goods line was sacrificed to create the space for the new platform 4 and restore some logic, as down trains would no longer have to cross over to use platform 3 all the time. The original station building seen here, constructed in 1842 to a Brunel design, has quite rightly been listed. Historic England states that it has 'a strong classical styling with characterful Swindon masonry and maintains an architectural presence of a scale uncommon amongst GWR railway stations'.

No. 43179 *Pride of Laira* tops the climb from the Severn Tunnel at Pilning with the 12.32 from Swansea to Paddington on 16 September 1994. Still on the incline, 43036 pushes the train, which is obscuring from our view the mile-long loop line here. The 1 in 100 climb out of the tunnel itself was a major challenge in the past but remains something to be reckoned with today, even when the driver has 4,500hp at his disposal. Brakes have to be applied gently on the way down into it in order to stay within the ruling 70mph restriction and then full power applied on the way out. Over the years, Pilning station had become of more use to railway enthusiasts than passengers, though even that has changed since the removal of its footbridge; now only eastbound trains can call there (since public access to the westbound side is no longer possible) and there are just two of those, Saturdays only!

LEFT The infamous fag packet livery! Smokers would need to confirm exactly which brand of cigarette comes closest to it (would it be Superkings?), although the fine lines and gold band probably have a lot to do with it. And it certainly wasn't a bad livery. However, a cruel nickname may possibly not have helped its longevity and First Great Western were looking to replace it fewer than five years from its first application. On 30 June 2001, an up express sweeps across the gently rolling landscape at Oath, fringing Sedgemoor in Somerset, on a stretch of main line that is said to be the longest in the country without a station – 28 miles between Taunton and Castle Cary. It's a warm and sunny afternoon, so one passenger has elected to stand by an open window at the front of first class. The Mark 3s were the last design of long-distance rolling stock in this country to have any window that a passenger could choose to open. With the passenger saloon being air conditioned, this could present problems during especially hot or cold weather but many appreciated the chance to sample some real fresh air during a journey, or to grab a quick puff of a cigarette when the train conductor wasn't about. Sadly, it also led to some avoidable injuries and worse over the years.

RIGHT Severn Tunnel Junction has essentially been reduced to what you see here and using a minimum number of switches. The once-sprawling marshalling yards have disappeared beneath three decades of tree growth and a new stretch of the M4, built to serve the Second Severn Crossing in 1996. Second of the production power cars, 43003 *Isambard Kingdom Brunel* has swung towards the tunnel approaches with the seven-coach 12.28 Swansea to Paddington service on 3 August 2012. How remarkable that such an old machine should be deemed worthy of further service in Scotland, forty-two years after it was introduced to the Western Region. The building seen in the background above the first coach was the small servicing shed for the loco stabling point and the writer well remembers walking down the middle of two long lines of class 37s, 47s and 'Peaks' here late one Sunday evening in the 1980s, collecting their numbers as their air systems clicked and hissed away at him in the gloom. As coal and freight traffic generally declined, BR decided that it could dispense with the facilities here, apart from the small unmanned station. Since the overhead wires have been erected, it looks different again today. St Mary's Church tower in Rogiet village has seen it all.

Go West – Ways out West

ABOVE Almost forgotten perhaps at one extremity of the network is Pembroke Dock station. The town was an important base for flying boats during the last war and now has a developing heritage centre but with just a single line to a single platform, its chances of hosting any kind of charter train are currently nil. The station building itself has recently undergone a sympathetic restoration of its glazed roof canopies; after a small further investment to the track capacity, perhaps more people could be encouraged to visit Pembrokeshire by train in future. The country needs more coastal resorts that can be *comfortably* visited by train, in other words not just on a DMU with no leg room or luggage capacity! Providing an example of what can be achieved, on Saturday, 22 July 2017, 43187 (carrying 'Welsh Dragon' transfers) has arrived from Swansea and will shortly trail the 10.04 departure to London Paddington with 43155 *The Red Arrows – 50 Seasons of Excellence* heading it back up the branch. *Clive Hanley*

RIGHT Perhaps this isn't the most remarkable photograph of the first production power car (43002 at Exeter St David's on 9 July 1985) but it shows the very nameplate that caused all kinds of controversy when first unveiled: *Top of the Pops*. Many will recall the indignant letters written to railway journals in the aftermath of the naming event on live television on 30 August 1984, but for British Rail that didn't matter; getting their premier train featured on prime-time TV was publicity that simply could not be bought. The actual naming took place at Bristol Temple Meads' platform 3, following a successful attempt to set a world record for a start-to-stop run with diesel traction – sixty-two minutes thirty-three seconds for the 117.5-mile journey from Paddington. With a 2+5 formation of vehicles (43003 being the other power car) and acceleration being applied at the earliest opportunity after all restrictions, maximum speed was never any higher than 128mph. The Chief Civil Engineer had arranged for all temporary speed restrictions to be lifted; indeed, the ride on board the train was said to be exemplary. It's fair to say that the risk taken making the record attempt in such a high-profile manner had paid off handsomely, in front of an estimated 10 million viewers. The driver's name was Harry Rail. You really couldn't make it up. *Arthur Turner/Transport Treasury*

West (and East) of the Tamar

The pink doors of this HST arriving at Lostwithiel stand out in the bright sunshine of 23 April 2011. By this date, the re-equipping of HSTs with the MTU engine was complete and operators were benefitting from much-improved reliability. It would not be the first time that a particular breed of motive power achieved its best reliability figures in the run up to its rundown! The length of the train highlights the curvature of the line in addition to a marked change in gradient. The main line through Cornwall is characterised by many such features, making the smooth driving of trains something of an art. It also makes life tricky for the track engineers, who have to install any new track with varying cants and transitions from one curve to the next. And then to maintain it! The civil engineer is kept busy with a large inventory of ageing bridges, viaducts and embankments as the line negotiates its path through such a varied countryside. As for this power car, 43145 led a fairly uneventful life on the Western and without receiving a name. Latterly, it resides in Scotland and works out of Haymarket depot.

RIGHT No. 43022 heads an up service to Paddington on a glorious spring morning at East Largin Viaduct on 19 April 2013. This clean blue train stands out well among its surroundings of leafless trees, although many were affected by some kind of blight and were about to be cut down. According to the British Listed Buildings website, this viaduct sits upon 'eight piers of rusticated snecked slate from Westwood Quarry (nearby)'. And very nice it looks too, even after standing proud since 1886, when the original timber trestle affair was replaced after thirty years of use. A single line has pertained here since 1964, when it was felt that the viaduct should no longer be expected to handle the simultaneous passage of two heavy trains. The lonely Largin signal box, which guarded this short single line section until 1992, had to be supplied with drinking water from passing trains and was situated on the curve beyond the viaduct. The Cornwall Railway Society's website provides a lot of detail and stories about the railway in this area and is recommended reading.

LEFT Even though their HSTs were entering their final phase of long-distance service, some vehicles were given the all-over green livery treatment to accompany the rebranding of the franchise as 'Great Western Railway'. Going for heritage appeal can work for certain products but possibly not with trains, in the writer's opinion. In running a twenty-first-century service, the railways should be looking forward, not back. Furthermore, a green train passing through green countryside does not really make the best of impressions. On 7 May 2016, 43187 leaves Plymouth for Paddington as an illustrious predecessor sits in the station alongside a Cross Country set. Diesel hydraulic D1015 *Western Champion* had earlier come down from London with Pathfinder Tours' 'Western Challenger' non-stop special.

HST – The Train That Saved Britain's Railways

Torquay was enjoying hot weather on 29 June 2018 as 43086 called there on its way down to Paignton. The driver takes the opportunity to stretch his legs, though journey's end is close at hand. Attempts to make the vacant space between the tracks here a touch more interesting have clearly been made in the past, though I suspect that draconian rules forbidding station staff from leaving the platform have served to put an end to that. The 'one size fits all' approach to safety shouldn't be the answer to everything.

And so to the River Tamar itself on 26 May 2017. With me travelling back in first class from a holiday on the Isles of Scilly (if you've never been there, you should go!), 43037 *Penydarren* is easing the 13.03 Penzance to Paddington onto the Royal Albert Bridge at Saltash. I am taking advantage of the ability to lean out of a train window (briefly!) to take a photograph like this before all chances of doing so vanish forever. The slight hogging of the bridge decks is quite evident from this angle. After crossing the bridge, I settled back into my leather-upholstered seat to enjoy the ride home and the complimentary snacks. What a shame there was no travelling chef on board! This may well have been the last time that I would have travelled on a regular-timetabled High Speed Train at 125mph.

One year later finds me on holiday in Devon again and walking the footway across the Tamar road bridge, providing as it does a grand spectacle of the older structure. This view, taken on 30 June 2018, nicely illustrates how Brunel's masterpiece cradles the train as it passes high above the water beneath. I wrote this caption shortly after seeing the bridge featured in Tim Dunn's very watchable TV series *The Architecture the Railways Built*. He likes his HSTs as well, so he deserves a mention! I'm afraid I was concentrating too much on getting the photograph to note the number of this power car at the head of its Paddington-bound train.

Another visit to Devon means one more opportunity to see long-distance HSTs operating for Great Western through the county before the class 800 takeover is complete. On 13 September 2018, 43190 is digging into the climb of Rattery Bank, which faces all westbound trains from the moment they leave Totnes station. The advent of twin-powered HSTs with their fixed formations apparently ended concerns about trains climbing the fearsome gradients of Rattery, Dainton or Hemerdon. However, the loss of a single power car during the low-adhesion season still presented headaches for drivers on occasion. Since the availability of any spare locomotive in the area to assist a train in trouble is now effectively zero, the stop at Totnes could be omitted to assist with the train's momentum. Or the service terminated and passengers put onto buses instead, of course. Although an HST power car might have a similarly rated horsepower to a Warship diesel from the 1960s, it is geared for higher-speed running and therefore does not have the low down torque to keep a heavy load slowly on the move up a steep gradient. The head shunt behind the train was once used during the sorting of milk tankers that served the dairy beside the station. The chimney beyond, constructed by Brunel for his atmospheric railway pumping station, was in the dairy complex and came under threat of demolition after its closure in 2007.

Cross Country HSTs continue to run into the West Country at the time of writing. No. 43207 brings 1S52 12.25 Plymouth–Edinburgh into the up station loop at Totnes, also on 13 September 2018. This view is looking back to the bridge from which 43190 was photographed and has an equally hilly backdrop on display; the two trains probably met in Plymouth station about half an hour beforehand. Two features of note on the track are the TPWS grids in the 'four foot' next to signals E198 and E98 together with several glued rail joints. TPWS (Train Protection and Warning System) was rolled out in the early 2000s at signals that were judged to be at heightened risk from SPADs. This term, Signal Passed At Danger, grabbed itself a place in the public consciousness following the tragic Ladbroke Grove collision where a red signal was passed and nothing was left to prevent the offending multiple unit from continuing on to disaster. The TPWS applies brakes on a train that passes these signals at danger; others do so if they detect a train is approaching a signal at danger too quickly to stop or a speed restriction too fast. Also, glued insulated rail joints are installed where track circuiting is used for train detection, the glue being applied to make the joints more robust in track where train speeds or loadings are higher.

Where the Rails Meet the Sea

Used for publicity purposes since the days of the Great Western Railway, the view of the railway at Horse Cove, near Dawlish, is very well known. Railway photographers used to make the effort to walk out to it on sunny afternoons (off the South West Coast footpath) and would usually be rewarded with some pleasing results, regardless of what train came along. Sadly, nobody at Network Rail seemed to appreciate this when they sanctioned yet another stretch of their steel fencing and normal photography is now very difficult. With a little thought, a perfectly safe view point could be erected here for some good public relations. Leeds (Neville Hill)-based 43045 *The Grammar School Doncaster AD1350* commands the 09.43 York–Paignton on Saturday 22 June 1996 (43055 *Sheffield Star* is at the rear), as this set foregoes its normal duties on the Midland Main Line for a day. The cliff edge thrift has helped to bring a nice splash of colour into the left of shot.

Walking in the other direction from Dawlish station takes you along the top of the sea wall, of course. It is a stretch that is busy with walkers practically all year round, though perhaps not when there is a strong easterly wind blowing; a storm coming from that direction was to breach the wall in the vicinity of the rear portion of this train in February 2014, leaving both tracks hanging in mid-air. On 7 April 2010, 43301 heads a Plymouth-bound working along the backs of the houses of Riviera Terrace. The scaffolding erected outside two of the properties here demonstrates that the effect of stormy weather requires frequent attention to their facades. This particular power car itself suffered from a degree of neglect and (when numbered 43101) it was laid up for several years in the mid-2000s after its use on Virgin Cross Country services came to an end. So much so, that withdrawal from service was seriously considered; however, the transfer of Cross Country to Arriva in 2008 heralded a reprieve and an overhaul, a new MTU engine and renumbering saw it return to front-line service with other stored units. It had been decided that the much-vaunted Voyagers could not cope with the heavier service loadings that were becoming more frequent.

RIGHT We are now the other side of the footbridge visible in the background of the previous view, and the weather has changed a little, though not to the stormy extent described earlier. I am using Rockstone footbridge as an occasional shelter from the waves as they break over the wall, leaving the footpath and railway soaking wet. Even without that, there is a constant feed of salty spray coming in across the beach, with precious few walkers brave enough to enjoy it. On 24 October 2006, and on hire to Virgin Cross Country to cover for an accident-damaged class 221 Voyager unit, comes Midland Mainline-liveried 43081. It was working a Derby–Plymouth–Newcastle–Derby diagram. Track-circuited signalling was tried along this stretch of railway for a time but the ever-present sea water splashing onto the line played havoc with the low current and an axle counter system soon replaced it. The up line was also configured for bi-directional working so that, in the event of inclement weather forcing the closure of the outer track, some form of service could be maintained. Be that as it may, very often the bad weather can require complete cessation of services.

LEFT The well-known vantage point here is the top of Langstone Rock, which may be a little tricky to conquer for those less capable. I wonder whether the erosion from people's feet may become of concern here at some point in the future. No. 43142 and 43174 *Bristol-Bordeaux* combine to work the 09.45 Plymouth–Paddington off the sea wall and around the corner to Dawlish Warren. On 28 August 2006, First Great Western's 'dynamic lines' livery was just being rolled out across their HST coaches, though it was not to find favour on the power cars for some reason; all of the latter ended up painted in solid blue. It was to be the end of the 'F in circle'! Reliability of the HST fleet was also said to have dropped around this period as heavier maintenance of the Valenta engines was cut back in anticipation of their re-engining with MTU power units. That was clearly putting passengers *second* rather than *first*!

At the top of the Rockstone footbridge on 25 September 2020, early evening sunshine illuminates the track beautifully for about half an hour or so before the shadows creep in too much. Common sense has prevailed and permitted HSTs some kind of afterlife on Great Western as they work in shortened formation on certain services between Cardiff and Penzance, based at Laira. No. 43093 *Old Oak Common HST Depot 1976-2018* heads 2C34 16.22 Exeter St David's–Penzance; the inset sliding doors on the coaches of these sets can be discerned. Over the years, the celebrated red sandstone cliffs at Dawlish have become progressively covered by more greenery and I'm not sure whether that is a good thing or not – does it help to protect the stone from erosion? Earlier on this day, a ceremony had taken place to mark the completion of the first stage of the wall reinforcement close to Dawlish station itself. Protecting the railway in this locality from the sea is clearly vital, but having an inland alternative route is equally important if a link to the South West is to be maintained in all weathers.

Dawlish Warren is a popular little resort in season with its amusements and fast food outlets. For any railway enthusiast tiring of those attractions, the first port of call may well be the footbridge at the south end of the station as it affords a good view in both directions. The majority of trains pass through the centre roads, as 43136 is seen doing leading its westbound train on a pleasantly warm 25 May 2012, but stopping trains make use of the platform loops; this sort of station layout used to be commonplace but today rates as being unusual. The eight camping coaches here have been in place for at least thirty years now, having replaced an older set of vehicles that had also served their time as somewhat different holiday accommodation. And where would Network Rail be without their Transit vans? One of their employees appears to be waiting for the go-ahead to carry out his next task for the day. But we can be certain he won't be trying to shift that discarded and rusty old crossover section without assistance. Note that the crossover rails themselves have track circuit continuity welding ('zigzag') to overcome the possibility of poor track circuit registering of train movements over this seldomly used facility.

Not strictly part of the sea wall section but when you are travelling down from London or Bristol, the stretch past Cockwood Harbour is something of a curtain raiser to what follows. Some photographers prefer to have water in the harbour here and most look back fondly to the time when there wasn't a fence along the track. But at least it wasn't made a solid wall. It is obviously a warm day here, judging by the fact that the driver of 43357 has the cab door open as his train heads up country on 23 September 2016. Notice that the nearest door of the front coach isn't picked out in red as this is only for the use of the train conductor. When their train proceeds along the line between here and Starcross, passengers are sometimes surprised to look across the Exe estuary to see another train on the other side because, of course, the Exmouth branch runs in parallel at a distance of less than 2 miles away.

On Location

This first interlude considers the terminus stations frequented by HSTs and the physical features that were once commonplace beside their tracks, both on and off the railway. Since the end of steam, previously only enthusiasts might have noticed the passage of a train in the landscape; the HST changed that.

Terminus Velocity

The flared trousers on display shout out '1970s' in this picture, taken before the Paddington 'Lawn' was extended. And not a single trolley case to be seen! It's 29 October 1979, so the Eighties are only weeks away, but the power car belonging to set 253027, in contrast to those from 030 and 021, has not yet been to the workshops to have its exhaust cowling fitted. In 1976, the earliest sets into traffic had the 'InterCity 125' legend painted in black (when black was expected to be the main livery colour on power cars), before blue with lettering outlined in white was settled upon. After crew training had taken place earlier on in that year's long and hot summer, the first HST services began in the August, the high speed timetable being due to start on 4 October. How interesting to see 'Dad' showing his two daughters the cab as the family arrive in the capital; so railways weren't only for the boys! With the High Speed Train, it could not be denied that passengers knew what sort of train they were getting on, regardless of how they approached it at a station; there was a streamlined locomotive at either end and every vehicle was labelled 'InterCity 125'. One early Western Region promotion offered reduced second-class fares on some trains, billed as '125mph for just 125 pence'. *Arthur Turner/Transport Treasury*

ON LOCATION – TERMINUS VELOCITY

RIGHT The first major modification to an HST power car came in 1987 as part of trials for the planned introduction of Driving Van Trailers to both the WCML and ECML. This involved the fitment of buffers to 43123 and then 43014 at the Railway Technical Centre in Derby. The new class 91s were designed from the outset with push-pull operation in mind but the TDM (Time Division Multiplex) control system was also going to be employed on WCML trains, with DVT vehicles reducing the locomotive requirement and generally speeding up turnarounds at Euston, in particular. No. 43123 (shown there in platform 6) began regular working on trains to the West Midlands in December 1987; it provided power to the coaches but motive power came entirely from the electric locomotive at the other end. With the reduction of yellow frontage under the nose, it was decided that additional yellow warning paint was needed around the windows to satisfy Railway Group Standards. The first four production power cars had originally been earmarked for buffer fitment prior to the ECML work: Nos 43002/3/4/5 received the same extra paint treatment from St Philip's Marsh depot.
Transport Treasury Archive

LEFT British Rail was so keen to make full use of the HST that spare sets were found to spread them onto West Coast Main Line services, working 'under the wires' in preference to using electric locomotive-hauled trains. During the last few months of their WCML turns, with Virgin Trains running them to Blackpool, 43100 waits in platform 7 at Euston on 29 January 2003. VT had even named this example *Blackpool Rock* for a time but by now its bodyside transfers had disappeared; actual nameplates were never carried. Platforms 6 and 7 at Euston were denoted for HST operation, presumably as the exhaust fumes could be better dispersed from there than in other platforms. The fitment of smoke alarms at certain stations around the network has led to electric train-only operating procedures put in place, leading to problems when an unexpected diesel unit pays a visit.

LEFT After the short reign of National Express as franchise holder for ECML long-distance services, a variety of livery styles took hold on the HST fleet. The government-run 'East Coast' franchise chose this grey livery for the power cars and left the coaches little changed. For some years, there was to be no uniform livery style across the whole fleet. Following completion of the station's total refurbishment in 2012, the clean and re-glazed roof allows plenty of sunlight onto 43257 as it sits in platform 4 at King's Cross on 18 July 2013. The coming of Eurostar services to St Pancras station next door also served to improve the feel of the whole area around King's Cross, which for far too long had held a reputation for seediness and a part of London to be avoided after dark.

RIGHT The driver for the next First Great Western departure finds the cab door of 43131 already open on 19 March 2010, suggesting that a technician is attending to his train. Technical riding inspectors spent their time moving from one set to the next throughout the day as, however good the overnight depot maintenance might be, there is no substitute for seeing how trains actually perform in service. A driver's first concern is the safe running of the train; faulty equipment is always an unwelcome distraction from that. This kind of platform end scene at Paddington played out over the decades but ended with the last HST departures on 18 May 2019. No. 43131 and 43150 alongside it both lost their names (*Sir Felix Pole* and *Bristol Evening Post*) in 2007, as did several others with FGW; these two are now part of the Scotrail fleet.

ON LOCATION – TERMINUS VELOCITY

The canted track at the country end of Paddington station allows trains to make a slightly faster getaway than would otherwise be the case; the ballast is treated with polymer to hold it together and notices forbid the use of tamping machines in that vicinity! The ruling limit past Royal Oak is 40mph, before the full 125mph prevails onwards to Reading. Mid-afternoon on 23 April 2010, the NMT (with 43013 and 43062 *John Armitt*) departs platform 11 for line 4 and then the down relief line, en route to Oxford and Derby, just as a service train pulls away on line 2. The track-level signal post telephones visible under the gantry (one of which seems to be leaning rather precariously) are all marked as only for use in emergencies, due to the insufficient clearances with the adjacent line.

LEFT When we're reminded of how it used to be, it does seem something of a pity that Midland Main Line services should have been completely banished from under the great roof of St Pancras in favour of Eurostar operations. No doubt passengers have appreciated the reduction in the noise levels, though! On 24 May 2002, MML on-train staff share a joke as passengers pick a door, any door, while a station employee takes a moment to lean upon his own allotted transport. No. 43044 will soon be spouting twin plumes of exhaust into the roof as the driver prepares his train for departure from platform 3. There was no platform 1 at this time since that had long been abolished but a station siding remained in the wide space between two and three. Such supplementary tracks were a throwback to the days when stock might be stabled there between duties, though there was always the interesting possibility of a failed locomotive finding itself parked there in disgrace; it all contributed to an interesting railway scene.

RIGHT Lastly in London, we pay a visit to the other terminus that received HSTs on a timetabled basis: Waterloo. No. 43125 *Merchant Venturer* is pictured there in platform 19 during February 1996 when Eurostar services connected with the Continent and daily HSTs were laid on to feed them from Manchester, Edinburgh and Cardiff. This was in anticipation of 'Regional' Eurostars linking those cities directly with Paris and Brussels. Unfortunately, the apparent convenience of these HSTs didn't appeal to sufficient Eurostar customers, who tended to opt for regular services and the London Underground to access Waterloo. One train from Cardiff was noted arriving with just twelve people on board, including the staff! The HST-operated services soon ended and the Regional Eurostars never even began operation. Those expensively constructed international platforms at Waterloo fell out of use for a number of years following the switch of Eurostars to St Pancras, but FGW HSTs would still revisit sometimes when engineering or emergencies led to their diversion from Paddington. *Graham Smith*

ON LOCATION – TERMINUS VELOCITY

We go north to some of the last termini in the country to witness HST operation. I found that Scotrail staff at Inverness were very happy to assist with my wish to obtain photos there, this being somewhat in contrast to experiences I've had over the years at certain English stations, particularly around London! Detail on the side of 43127, just arrived with the 07.00 from Glasgow Queen Street, highlights some of the landmark attractions that are features of the 'seven cities' served by Scotrail's HST fleet. These silhouettes feature scenes from Edinburgh, the William Wallace statue in Aberdeen, the Dundee Law Beacon War Memorial and the statue of Flora Macdonald beside Inverness Castle. On the other side are scenes from Glasgow, the Royal Scots Greys Monument in Edinburgh and the Wallace Monument and Castle at Stirling. Beyond 43127 is the Inverness and Nairn Railway's Lochgorm Works building from 1855, largely still performing the purpose for which it was originally intended.

The Signals Were There

The case for purchasing extra sets to work to Paignton and Penzance hadn't been an easy one for British Rail to make, when it was acknowledged that the trains would only achieve 125mph in the first 36 miles of their 200+ mile journeys. The presence of so many manually signalled sections proved a barrier to faster schedules until some major modernisation had been accomplished during the mid-1980s. On 28 August 1981, 43042 leads a Paddington–Plymouth service clear of Exeter St David's station (with 43031 at the rear). It is passing a gantry that was controlled from Exeter West box (beyond the third coach). Noteworthy is the fact that the central distant arm was controlled from Exeter Middle beside the Red Cow level crossing at the other end of the station, using the small electric motor mounted below it on the doll. Because it wasn't 'slotted' however, it needed the West box signalman to pull his own distant lever for it as well; something that would only occur in the comparatively rare event of a train passing through non-stop. Showing clearly on 43042 is the livery transition from its yellow 'power' section to the blue and grey of the guard's compartment that blended into the coaching stock. *Arthur Turner/Transport Treasury*

ON LOCATION – THE SIGNALS WERE THERE

RIGHT Several hundred miles north from Exeter is Blackford, on the main line between Perth and Stirling, where we find 43274 *Spirit of Sunderland* heading the diverted 09.10 Edinburgh to Aberdeen (with 43313 the trailing power car) on 14 February 2016. The usual route through Fife was closed on that day for engineering work. Down and up refuge sidings were still in place at this location and just beyond the signal box can be glimpsed what would be the last tall lattice post signal in Scotland to be abolished (in 2019). At the time of writing, the refuge sidings have been removed and a small freight terminal for the Highland Spring Group is being established. After decades of road dominance, it is to be hoped that more such enlightened organisations in the country will also make the move towards using rail transport for shipping their goods. *Ian Lothian*

LEFT A concerted effort is now currently under way to remove all lineside signalling from the railway network with the introduction of radio-based systems. Consequently, arrays of multiple-aspect signals (MAS) or colour lights such as these will also become a thing of the past. At the north end of Leicester station on 19 September 2006, 43166 waits to depart for Derby and Sheffield as 43066 (with 43056) arrives beneath the London Road bridge. Previously named *Nottingham Playhouse*, 43066 was one of a number of MML-based power cars to lose their names in premature fashion, seemingly as though one set of franchise management liked putting names on their trains while the next one didn't!

There is a different style about these colour light signals at Didcot. They have been placed higher up in the driver's sight lines, partly after a signal sighting committee would have met to decide on their placement, in the light of the coming electrification. On 2 December 2011, 43025 is working the 08.06 from Oxford to Paddington; it will soon be on its way to Reading with another load of commuters for the capital, once that other set has cleared the next signal section and it has been 'given the feather'. Maintenance of these signals, while clearly being less frequent than for traditional semaphores, still requires a safe means of access, hence the provision of a substantial gantry.

On Location – The Signals Were There

There have been many contrasts between old and new on Britain's railways over the years: From the Pannier Tanks that hauled maintenance trains on the London Underground in the 1970s to the 186mph Eurostar trains that cruised past the wooden gates of the keeper-operated level crossing at Willesborough in Kent. High Speed Trains encountered lower-quadrant semaphore signalling when their sphere of operation was extended to take in the West Country in late 1979. On 24 April 1984, 43180 is signalled towards Totnes at Aller Junction, just outside Newton Abbot. It is not only the wonderful array of semaphore signals that point to a bygone era hereabouts but the entirely wooden sleepered track. Three years later, the junction (behind the photographer) would cease to exist in a grand simplification of the tracks in the Newton Abbot district, coupled with new colour light signalling controlled from Exeter. Today, trains now have their route selected at the West Junction, which is a series of crossovers situated around the curve just out of shot. Perhaps more of a change is the improvement to the parallel main Torquay road (the A380), which is now a dual carriageway, putting paid to those lovely evergreen trees in the background, not to mention the farm bridge from which this view was taken. *Arthur Turner/Transport Treasury*

Towers of Strength

When I say 'towers', of course I'm referring to the cooling towers of this country's power stations and the strength they have provided to its economy for at least half a century; HSTs have been seen running past them for much of that time. The Midlands and the north of England had the greatest accumulation and the one at Ratcliffe on Soar sits to the south of Nottingham to this day. On an icy 29 November 1989, 43107 swings towards the largest city in the East Midlands at Trent South Junction with a down express, the power station clearly at full stretch. Commissioned in 1968, it came to be the largest consumer of coal mined in the area and was chosen for modification to make it more environmentally friendly in the 1990s. It will be one of the last of its kind when coal-fired generation of electricity in the UK is due to cease in 2024.

ON LOCATION – TOWERS OF STRENGTH

Looking from the other side, an up train on 7 June 2005 is headed by 43060 *County of Leicestershire* in what was by now the 'old' livery for Midland Mainline, the rest of this set (including trailing power car 43104) being in the replacement darker livery. It is a warm summer's afternoon but the cooling towers suggest that the station is quietly contributing baseload power to the National Grid. At one time, coal trains would be supplying Ratcliffe PS from the Toton yard direction round the clock. The difference in rail fastenings here between the down and up fast tracks is apparent: The down has the distinctive Pandrol clip dating from the 1960s, while the up has the less obtrusive 'Fastclip', whose design permits mechanical installation or removal. Today's rail network features fewer tracks that see more intensive use, so there is an ongoing drive to reduce the time it takes to maintain it.

53

On 2 December 2011, 43069 draws to a stand at Didcot with an up service to Paddington. It looks as though the driver has found another use for his copy of the *Metro* free newspaper, providing an enhancement to the sun visor on a very brightly lit winter's morning. The lady on the platform would seem to have a first-class ticket, judging by the direction she is walking. With only 53 miles to Paddington, she will have a little over half an hour to peruse that pile of documentation she is carrying – or even less if she's only going to Reading! Meanwhile, DMU 165119 waits nearby before making a slower run into the capital.

Didcot Parkway station used to be overshadowed by the power station next door to it but today its cooling towers are no more. It would quite simply never have functioned without the contribution of rail transport, supplying it with coal from the Midlands: MGR trains began feeding Didcot 'A' in 1970, using rakes of MGR wagons hauled mostly by class 47/3 diesels at first before they handed over to class 56s and 58s in the 1980s. Class 60s came to be employed on trains that brought imported coal via Avonmouth Docks in the 1990s, a change that required the reinstatement of relief lines between Wantage Road and Challow in order to avoid delaying the HSTs! Closure came in 2013 and the 200m-high chimney was the last major feature to be brought down with explosives in 2020; the online video of that event is remarkable, though sad to recall that four lives were lost during the earlier phase of demolition.

ON LOCATION – TOWERS OF STRENGTH

Moving to the north, Ferrybridge C Power Station provides the backdrop to this power car move for 43185 *Great Western* in InterCity 'Swallow' livery and 43002 *Sir Kenneth Grange* in original livery. The former had been specially repainted at Laira and was en route to York for an unveiling ceremony at the NRM. The Rail Operations Group was established in 2014 with an eye on special movements of rolling stock, something that was expected to pick up with the forecasted increase in the introduction of new train fleets and consequent retirement or reuse of older stock, among other developments. The date is 30 September 2016 and the photographer's camera was mounted on a pole. After a life of incident (including collapsing cooling towers and fires), the station had ceased generation earlier that year and now waits in silence for the demolition contract to be executed on its eight cooling towers and two chimneys. Journeys along the railway and the adjacent M62 and A1 motorways will seem to be missing something when they're gone. There may not be room in preservation for all celebrity-liveried HST power cars and 43185 has reportedly gone to supply spares for the Scotrail contingent. *Jason Rogers*

Train in the Landscape

I suppose this view of an HST crossing a high embankment on a midsummer's evening could have been taken in all kinds of places. It is the 19.45 Paddington to Bristol Temple Meads passing near to the village of Dauntsey in Wiltshire, with the time now 20.50 on 12 June 1992. The film used was Fujichrome 50 and the exposure 1/1,000sec at f2.8+½ (when I used to religiously record that kind of detail after every shot!).

My camera was a Minolta X500; not a bad camera, though the film would occasionally develop a crease across it if you left it in the camera for too long between outings. You had to remember to waste the first shot after winding it on if you didn't want a nice vertical band out of focus across the photo! Nowadays, photographers are spoilt by the amount of 'bells and whistles' that they find on their digital cameras.

ON LOCATION – TRAIN IN THE LANDSCAPE

On 5 August 1995, another sideways-on picture of an HST finds the first production power car 43002 rushing past the Alton Barnes White Horse near to Woodborough, bound for London. By this date, its *Top of the Pops* nameplates had been updated to the latest style, a kind of flatter stainless steel item in a very shiny finish that made it hard to read from certain angles. These plates attracted quite a bit of unflattering criticism and were all removed before they'd spent very long on these power cars and other locomotives generally. The livery of the train at least helps it to stand out from the countryside it is passing through, something that the current all-over green livery of Great Western does not do, as mentioned elsewhere.

This vista is looking down from Ash Lane, Almondsbury, towards the Second Severn Crossing, still under construction on 30 March 1996. A shaft of sunlight on an otherwise disappointingly cloudy day catches the 12.32 Swansea–Paddington HST leaving Pilning in its wake and heading for Patchway Tunnel on the outskirts of Bristol. The Western Region's fleet of trains were all extended to eight coaches in 1990, following the release of stock from the Eastern when electrification had created a surplus. Any depot facilities that had only been built to cater for 2+7 formations required some expensive upgrading, of course.

For a reasonably successful panned shot of a train, you need to find a stretch of track that is sufficiently raised and clear of vegetation where you have long enough to execute the all-important sweep of the camera. You need to have enough time to pick up the pace of the train and be moving the camera 'in sympathy' with it before it's immediately opposite your position, when you have to take the shot. A motor drive is invaluable here: you fire a burst of three or four and hopefully one will be OK. If you only take a single shot, the danger is that your pressing of the button will impart a vertical movement to the camera, producing an unwanted vertical blur in the shot. Shutter speeds need to be no faster than 1/80 second in my experience, preferably 1/60. You have to experiment and digital photography allows you to do that, of course. For this panned shot of a Paddington-bound train, I'd discovered a convenient patch of waste ground at Milton Park, to the west of Didcot. There's plenty of foreground and backdrop that can be blurred to enhance the speed effect. Also helping to create impact is the low autumn sunlight (the time was 09.00 and the date, 30 November 2011); this has served to highlight the driver of 43028, upright in his seat and casting a shadow onto the back of his cab.

RIGHT Brunel's Maidenhead Bridge is an engineering marvel. Completed in 1838, its arches are remarkably flat and it is no surprise that onlookers and commentators of the time shook their heads in disbelief that it would remain standing, let alone carry the weight of trains. Widened to take four tracks in the 1890s (by direction of another famous engineer, Sir John Fowler), it now carries express trains at up to 125mph and freight trains of several thousand tons on a daily basis. On 1 May 2018, the 13.22 London Paddington to Worcester Foregate Street is headed by 43144. A visit to inspect the 'Sounding Arch' from the River Thames path (over which this train is passing) is recommended, if only to test the echo.

LEFT Further along the route that the previous train would have taken, we are now on one of the most scenic stretches of the 'Cotswold Line' from Oxford to Worcester, as record breaker 43159 descends from Campden Tunnel towards Honeybourne in the Vale of Evesham. The specific location is Mickleton and the working is 1W27 13.22 Paddington–Worcester Foregate Street once more. North of Oxford, this service gathered a bit of a reputation for poor timekeeping and on 21 June 2018, true to form, was running around thirty minutes late. The redoubling of 20 miles of this route in 2011 enabled a more frequent service to be run. However, the single-track remnants at either end still serve to prevent recovery of the timetable whenever late running of just one service should occur. It's an example of how skimping on a project can lead to a longer-term loss of potential benefit.

It is often said that eastern England is characterised by 'big skies'; this is perhaps another way of saying it is rather flat. The cloud formations in this shot serve to emphasise the point somewhat as 43308 (and 43206) streak past Claypole village, south of Newark, on 24 August 2011 with 1D21, the 16.03 King's Cross to Leeds train. To the right of the railway fence must be one of the most photographed rusty farm trailers in the land, such is the popularity of this location with railway photographers! *Bill Atkinson*

ON LOCATION – TRAIN IN THE LANDSCAPE

Let's conclude this section with a look at the 'Flying Banana' as it cuts through the landscape at Churchdown, near Gloucester with the Malvern Hills in the distance. No. 43062 is in charge up front, though this time sporting a bit of self-promotion with the slogan 'Improving Your Railway', just for the benefit of rail users who didn't know what Network Rail might be doing running their own train around. Headcoded 1Z20, it would have left Reading Depot at 04.10 on the morning of Friday, 26 June 2020 and gone first to Swansea, before running up to Derby via Bristol Parkway. More than eight years after my last shift working aboard this train, I discovered that two of my former colleagues were manning the monitoring equipment on this occasion; they can just be made out sitting in the second coach above the NR logo.

Motive Power Matters

Since the dawn of railways, the locomotive has largely been a train's prime mover. The HST helped modify that somewhat by bringing the concept of the power car into the British railway mainstream. It was essential that its design should be an impressive one, if the whole train was to make the desired impact on the travelling public. It still looks modern after nearly half a century.

At the Double

We're at the country end of the old St Pancras station on 24 May 2002 as 43043 waits the last few seconds before departure with a Sheffield-bound train; the theatre box route indicator states 'F' for Fast line, as it normally would. I was about to board the other train with 43064 at the front, which would be going to Nottingham. As mentioned elsewhere, the lining out of these trains was clearly not done in a consistent fashion. The orange lines on 43064 would appear to be higher than those on 43043 – were tape measures not issued to workshop staff? I'm also inclined to wonder whether the pinkish paint used on those bridge girders was the same variety used on the Forth Bridge at the time. The engineer's support trolley will doubtless hold coolant for the thirstier Valenta engines that might call by – something of an Achilles heel with those power units for much of their life.

RIGHT Split-second timing on the part of the photographer has captured Executive-liveried 43039 and 43152 dashing past each other at Abbots Ripton on 31 March 1988. This stretch of the ECML suffered from the short-sighted decision to abolish several miles of the up slow line and then erect OHL stanchions in the space vacated. The reason why the provision for possible restoration of this track wasn't made is probably lost in the mists of time (or possibly dumped in the skip at privatisation). Network Rail's Huntingdon to Woodwalton scheme to re-quadrify this section has unfortunately been shelved. The surviving down slow is still made up of jointed track, though it must be in a good state of repair to sustain the ruling 80mph line limit. *Bill Atkinson*

LEFT The platforms at Birmingham New Street have never been the most attractive railway location but after dark, the character of the place changes somewhat. Following the less than successful advent of the Voyagers on Virgin's Cross Country routes in 2002, it was decided that four 2+5 HST sets would be retained for Birmingham to Manchester services until the spring of the following year. A five-second exposure records 43086 and 43193 *Plymouth, Spirit of Discovery* in platforms 1 and 2 at 18.15 on Saturday, 7 December 2002 while working two such trains. A plan to overhaul a small fleet of HSTs as class 255 'Challenger' sets (including these two power cars) was drawn up for some new routes, in addition to the core services being turned over to Voyagers. Their shortened formation would help fit into the accelerated timings applied to the Voyagers but the plan was dropped through lack of money. The paintwork on 43086 looks particularly tired.

Before the departure of the 15.10 to Leeds on 29 October 2007, the driver of (appropriately) 43053 *Leeds United* steps from the cab to make some last checks of his high-speed steed, just as a colleague enters King's Cross driving 43051. 'Discover Other Worlds with GNER' said the advertising on the latter, referring to the Tutankhamun exhibition at the O2 arena. Signalled out of the terminus on line B, the Leeds train will take the centre bore of Gasworks Tunnel and continue on to the down fast as it enters Copenhagen Tunnel. As service frequencies were stepped up and class 91 availability levels ebbed and flowed, East Coast drivers had long been trained on both HSTs and class 91s in order to maximise flexibility in crew rostering.

LEFT At Trent East Junction on 23 October 2003, two similarly mixed up formations appear alongside one another as both undertake some unusual duties: 43079 is coming off the Erewash Valley route with a Manchester Piccadilly–London St Pancras train; these services were intended as a stopgap during the worst of the disruption caused by the WCML upgrade. Meanwhile, 43089 waits in the goods loop during a special reversal that was required to turn the set on its way to Derby. It may well have come from Derby to begin with and was using the triangle of lines here to perform the manoeuvre; my recollection was that trains had to go down to Loughborough first as signalling did not permit a reversal at Trent South. No. 43078 was at the other end of this train but I did not record 43079's partner. Stencilled speed limit signs were becoming something of a rarity by this time! There was once a station at Trent with an island platform but the layout here has changed out of all recognition since its closure in 1968, helping to raise the line limit for expresses to or from the Nottingham direction.

ABOVE Two very clean First Great Western power cars sit beside one another at the south end of Bristol Temple Meads station on 8 April 2008. A substantial heat haze above 43145 on the left suggests that it is soon to leave for Paddington, while 43138 on platform 15 would appear to have been shut down after arriving from there; 37218 is in the stabling siding with a Network Rail test train. At this time, FGW operated fifty-three HST sets with 117 power cars, making it comfortably the largest operator of the train. Their £80 million refurbishment plan for the power cars was coming to its conclusion and not only involved the fitment of new engines but a redesigned cab layout too – something that was also being rolled out across the other operators' fleets. Improvements to FGW services in general were coming not a moment too soon after the operator had been voted the worst in the country by passengers and a service improvement notice had been issued by the Transport Secretary.

Motive Power Matters – At the Double

On 6 August 2016, electrification of the Great Western Main Line was well under way at some places along the route but Sonning Cutting was still escaping the attentions of the engineers, bar some vegetation reduction. I was not alone in taking photographs of trains here on this fine summer Saturday. Recalling some of the iconic images captured down in this famous cutting in the past, I did wonder whether anyone had thought to arrange for some images to be obtained before the wires changed the scenery for good. Perhaps not! British Rail had its own photographic unit and that would certainly have been active in the locality. But at least plenty of photos were being taken from above, including this of two eight-car sets passing each other between the London Road and Warren Road bridges: 43124 is at the rear of 1A14 11.00 Bristol–Paddington while 43040 *Bristol St Philip's Marsh* heads 1C13 12.00 Paddington–Bristol.

Come in Number 67 (Your Time For a Repaint)

Power car number 43067 has probably enjoyed one of the more varied experiences among its peers. A little over eighteen months into its BR service, it is shown sporting its unit number of 254006 at Hatfield on 10 April 1979 while operating a King's Cross–Leeds train. The highest shutter speed on most SLR cameras of the day was 1/1,000 second, but even that could be insufficient to stop the front of an HST at full speed from being slightly blurred. Noticeable on this rake of stock are the two red-lined sections denoting separate restaurant and buffet facilities for both first- and second-class passengers. Catering seemed to be all things to all men at first, from seeking to provide sit-down restaurant dining to a buffet bar in which drinkers might enjoy a beer, as if they were in a pub. Hardly surprisingly, this led to congestion in the aisles at times, along which a catering trolley was also expected to visit any passengers who were reluctant to leave their seats. Pressure to provide more seating generally and a preference for 'fast food' eventually led to reduced facilities and staff. *Arthur Turner/Transport Treasury*

RIGHT Into the 1980s finds 43067 working in the opposite direction, tailing the 11.45 out of Leeds station to London. After the launch of the new 'Executive' livery in 1983, power cars would receive their new colours more quickly than the stock, so this sort of arrangement was a relatively common sight, even four years later on 19 May 1987. The Eastern Region ditched the concept of set numbers early on and power car numbers took their place, sometimes under the windscreen like this or on the hatch cover below the nose. *Mick Barstow*

LEFT After its early years spent pounding up and down the ECML, 43067 first became marked out for different things when in 1988, along with five others, it was equipped with buffers as part of a plan to speed up the use of the overhead wires on the newly electrified parts of that route (43014 and 43123 had already been so modified for DVT trials). The new class 91s were ready but their mark 4 coaches were not, so these electrics were joined to existing HST sets of mark 3s with one power car removed and a buffer-fitted example at the other end (in case coupling up was required), as illustrated here. It's the first day of June 1989 and once more our 43067 is on a train to Leeds, but this time it is trailing into Doncaster station with electric loco 91004 out of sight up front. The latest InterCity 'Swallow' livery is now applied. *Arthur Turner/Transport Treasury*

Passing to the Cross Country sector and then Virgin Trains (upon privatisation), 15 April 2004 finds 43067 arriving at Stoke-on-Trent with a service to Manchester Piccadilly (with 43094), while now based at Laira. Judging by its oil-stained flank, it was perhaps not in the best of health! The centre road at Stoke had recently been relaid with new track but, rather oddly, this was to be removed again only a couple of years later. It was good to see a red-jacketed member of platform staff here, always ready to help passengers. At another large station (not too far away), some gained a reputation for disappearing whenever there was major disruption to the service!

LEFT A short spell with GNER followed later in 2004, after Virgin had completely (and mistakenly, in my opinion) divested itself of the High Speed Train in favour of their new Voyagers. On 12 October 2004, I was killing time on Edinburgh Waverley station when our subject quietly passed through on one of the non-platform roads, making a short test run from Craigentinny and presumably using the Edinburgh District line in the process. It is passing a water-jetting train powered by 37709 and 37886. No. 43067 performed for little more than three months in dark blue, as it was to be returned to store once more by the end of that year before finding short-term use again in 2005 …

BELOW … this time for Network Rail on the NMT. With those buffers, it could have proved a better choice for the test train than 43062 was, though other considerations came into play at the time the NMT's power cars were selected in 2002. Fresh after its repaint at Neville Hill, on 19 July 2005 the power car squeals around the sharp curve into Etches Park depot from Derby station's pilot siding, prior to working the monitoring train with 43154. Owing to the short-term hire of this unit, cameras were not fitted; only a simple paint job was carried out with no lining out and a smaller NR logo applied.

RIGHT No. 43067 saw use with the NMT for about six months before it was replaced by 43196. It went back into storage yet again for a while before the nascent open access operator Grand Central purchased it, along with 43065/68/80/84/123 (all buffer fitted) and it underwent overhaul at DML Devonport in Plymouth. I was driving down to Devon for a short holiday on 22 September 2007 when I passed this assemblage on the A38 dual carriageway going the other way. Noticing which power car it was, I realised I had to try to get a photo of it and turned the car around at the earliest opportunity without any real idea of how I might achieve that. Luckily, the truck was still having to climb up to Haldon Hill – the summit of the road – so having overtaken it easily enough I settled on this service area as the best place to park up and get the shot. The driver had clearly spotted what I was up to. Fish and chips for £6.99 would have been welcome at another time but I had a journey to complete after this; oh, but those roadside Little Chefs are sadly missed now!

LEFT Along with the NMT, GC's HST fleet was serviced at Heaton and I would often find one of the black sets sat about the depot as I was starting one of my own shifts there. The addition of the orange stripe made a big difference to the appearance of these trains, as solid black on its own was hardly an eye-catching livery. First-class section doors were picked out in gold, while standard were painted silver, most of these mark 3 vehicles having begun life as buffer-fitted stock that had previously been loco-hauled. By 11 April 2011, 43067 had become 43467 to demonstrate its re-equipment with the MTU engine.

Grand Central subsequently went for the all-DMU option for their services and one has to suspect it was for cost reasons; the class 180s that they chose to use instead have never enjoyed a good reputation for reliability and, as any seasoned traveller will tell you, a long journey on a train with 'head end power' is *always* better than one with engines under the floor (though the latest Hitachi trains are a significant improvement in that regard). So 43467 moved on to its next operator, this time being East Midlands Trains. It was honoured with a dual naming when the following plates were received at a ceremony in tribute to the emergency services, after the Nottingham station fire in January 2018: *British Transport Police Nottingham* and *Nottinghamshire Fire and Rescue Service*. Seen passing Cossington, it displays a modified version of the Stagecoach livery on 22 June 2018 while powering the 1C92 Derby–St Pancras service, formed of just six coaches. *Ben Wheeler*

Oh dear, its change of franchise time again, so another change of livery has to be made – just what was wrong with the old one? This very plain effort could not be described as an improvement (though possibly just the previous vinyls were removed) and as for the company name, hmm … 43467 heads for St Pancras International near Millbrook on 18 September 2020. The last remaining chimneys of the closed Stewartby brickworks complex may be seen beyond the rear of the train. Just above the trees on the left, a chimney of the modern era has been erected to serve the controversial new 'Rookery South' waste incinerator plant. Many of the exhausted clay pits in the area have since been filled with domestic refuse and power can be generated from the gas that is produced by it.

'And finally'.... This is expected to be the livery when it is applied to our intrepid power car sometime in 2021/22. Should a different colour scheme be tried in the event, then so be it! Working in partnership with Hanson and Hall, railadventure are a European rail company (based in Munich) now looking to begin operating in Britain. They have stated that they intend to use the six buffer-fitted power cars they've bought in pairs, effectively as three locomotives. 43467 will be paired up, as 43480 and 43484 have been already and will receive its EVN (European Vehicle Number) of 92 70 0043 467-4. '92' is a diesel loco code, '70' indicates that it is based in Britain, '0043' is the class and '467' the individual serial number. Last of all is the slightly curious 'check digit', a cunning means of checking for correct entry of the whole number into railway information systems: a mathematical calculation is performed by the computer on the first eleven numerals and the resultant figure should be the check digit. *Hanson and Hall*

Diesels on Depots

On Christmas Day 1989, our keen photographer has taken advantage of the annual network shutdown to obtain this view of HSTs taking a rare moment to rest at St Philip's Marsh depot. No. 43003 is the nearest power car. The discarded materials in the foreground would not be tolerated around any maintenance facility such as this today. Towards the close of the 1980s, the High Speed Train was entering a period when it would be worked harder than ever. Following the investment that had been made in East Coast electrification, little further money could be expected for new rolling stock. *Arthur Turner/Transport Treasury*

RIGHT Little information is available for this image. However, it is believed to be around August 1990 and the scene is at Bristol Bath Road depot. No. 43123 has been caught mid-shunt, away from the normal haunt for HSTs at St Philip's Marsh. A full repaint would appear to be the main reason, judging by the silver buffers plus the absent headlamp covers and horn grilles. The removal of the extra internal equipment required for DVT operation may also have taken place to standardise the unit in readiness for its next role, working cross-country services. Photos of HSTs with shiny buffers like this must be something of a rarity.
Transport Treasury Archive

LEFT Now we are at the aforementioned St Philip's Marsh depot (SPM), where 43128 is undergoing a load bank test of its electrical equipment on 23 March 2001. When the HSTs were first launched on the Western Region, this was one of only two depots fully equipped to service the new trains, the other being Old Oak Common (OOC). Any sets not stabled overnight at Cardiff or Swansea could be tripped to SPM. However, the large fuel capacity inherent in the specification enabled diagrams incorporating a night away from the main depot to be drawn up, so only basic cleaning and watering facilities were required in Wales. Landore depot (Swansea) ultimately became re-equipped to maintain power cars.

During 2003, Etches Park depot at Derby saw a concentration of HST sets from various train operators requiring the attention of Maintrain (the incumbent rolling stock maintainer), not only those belonging to Midland Mainline. This served to produce a chance coming together of five different liveries in a row in the carriage sidings during the afternoon of 20 May: 43180 is on the far left (displaying the latest MML livery), 43054 is alongside it (in the outgoing style), 43013 comes next on the recently formed New Measurement Train, then comes stranger in the camp First Great Western's 43009 (on loan) and lastly ex-Virgin 43086 (which had just arrived as empty stock). I had been inside the NMT observing preparations for the train's initial test runs when I noticed the Virgin set approaching; with camera at the ready in my kitbag, I quietly (but hastily!) moved to this position in readiness for what I hoped would be a unique shot. The next occasion I saw such a varied line-up was at the St Philip's Marsh Open Day, some thirteen years later.

ABOVE We are now looking across almost to the place where I was stood for the previous photograph, as this is a view from the Deadman's Lane side of the depot. On 5 April 2005, 43062 ticks over to provide power to the NMT set, most of which is inside the servicing shed of Etches Park to enable the Network Rail support staff to maintain their monitoring kit. MML's 43047 sits among rolling stock that has all acquired the new MML livery; it was probably one of the last in the old style by this time. Notice the well-maintained walkways and tidy sidings with ample yellow-painted board crossings to ensure staff safety.

RIGHT In the same year, we find two GNER sets in the sidings at Neville Hill Depot (Leeds) on 3 July: 43112 *Doncaster* is in the centre, with an unidentified class 91 loco showing its 'blunt' end to the camera and 43118 *City of Kingston upon Hull* prominent in the foreground with a striking experimental headlamp style. This latter modification was not adopted for the fleet fitment of the LED headlamps that followed. The trend towards using much brighter headlamps on trains sparked off quite a debate at the time, with many drivers especially unhappy at finding themselves dazzled by oncoming trains – were train headlights principally to *see* (lineside notices, for example) or to *be seen* (by track workers)? *Phil Marsh*

The New Measurement Train hosted perhaps its most visible test of trialled equipment when Hitachi teamed up with Brush and Porterbrook Leasing to equip it with a hybrid traction package, all with an eye to a greener future. No. 43089 was released from the MML fleet to be modified to run on battery power at low speed, charging up during regenerative braking. However, to allow the power car to be easily reconfigured back to its normal diesel-only operation, the batteries were fitted into their own support vehicle, converted mark 3 coach 977996 (formerly TGS 44062). Under a somewhat threatening sky, 30 April 2008 finds the experimental combination at the north end of the NMT rake, while stabled between ECML duties at Ferme Park in North London. The batteries relieved the diesel from its most inefficient phase during acceleration from rest, gradually passing control of the drive around the 20mph mark. No. 43089 *Hayabusa* carried a metal Falcon crest on its side, rather like another experimental Brush diesel from the 1960s did, though it was not retained on re-conversion back to a standard unit again; its interesting history has perhaps contributed towards its preservation with the 125 Group.

Motive Power Matters – Diesels on Depots

LEFT Also at Neville Hill but eight years later on, we see this headless apparition on 25 July 2009. *Sans* driving cab, 43061 has been shunted well clear of the power car maintenance bays and will be called up again in due course. The modular design of the HST in general was undoubtedly one of its strengths, giving rise to quicker turnarounds from repairs and therefore greater availability for traffic. Few railway assets have ever been 'sweated' so much in service to produce the maximum return on their original investment, in Britain at least.

RIGHT Heaton depot in Newcastle took responsibility for the maintenance of Grand Central's train fleet, both HST sets and class 180 'Adelante' DMUs. The latter have proved to be a somewhat disappointing successor to the HST, even considering their lower running costs. With their termination of HST operations, GC now have the majority of the class 180s in their fleet (ten). As far as number 43484 is concerned, it began BR service as 43084 in set 254015 during February 1978 and went on to receive its buffers (for DVT operations) at Stratford Works in 1988. It acquired an MTU power unit in 2010, together with this new number, and is seen on 11 April 2011. After latterly spending time in the EMR fleet, at the time of writing it is at Eastleigh in preparation for use with new operator 'railadventure'. To my mind, it's those wheeled toolboxes that make this photograph. Heaton received the first High Speed Train vehicles allocated to East Coast services, in late 1977.

There has never been a full HST maintenance depot at the London end of the Midland route itself, only this stabling facility at Cricklewood sidings; a couple of HST sets could often be seen here during the day in preparation for the evening rush homeward. No. 43046 is seen lined up there with one of the 'supporting act' on 10 May 2013 – well, have the Meridians genuinely served as a worthy successor to the HSTs? Let's just say that I cannot see the Bombardier Voyager/Meridian design being so fondly remembered thirty-plus years from now. That enormous gap to accommodate the automatic coupling unit hasn't done it any favours in the styling direction, it must be said.

ABOVE This is a sight that I saw many times at Old Oak Common as I started or finished a working shift on the NMT. However, that would usually be very early in the morning or late at night; this view on 28 June 2011 was taken mid-morning because I had been on site to undergo a depot induction refresher course. No. 43037 and 43196 are clearly the first two power cars here, plugged into the shore supply inside the servicing shed, though four more are in line parked behind the yellow stop boards hanging from the roof. The blue tub in the foreground holds a toilet treatment chemical – most important stuff!

RIGHT A slight variation on the 'Swallow' theme applied after privatisation, albeit quite short-lived, was an application of extra red and grey sections around the cab area of number 43028. This was part of the tranche of Virgin West Coast rolling stock allocated to North Wales route services from Euston, which connected with sailings between Holyhead and Dublin. The extra colour was thought to be a nod to the Irish CIE's locomotive livery and is shown in the process of being applied at Longsight depot in Manchester on 17 July 1997. *Bob Sweet*

The Fame of the Nose

It is beyond question that the nose design has helped make the High Speed Train stand out as the transport phenomenon that it is. While the prototype train certainly had a futuristic look about it, the decision to markedly improve upon it for the production train paid dividends: Sir Kenneth Grange's more raked-back profile, crucially permitted to dispense with the problem of buffers, has stood the test of time. Imagine this late Seventies line-up at the country end of Paddington station with four sets of buffers on show as well; it simply wouldn't have provided the same degree of impact to the onlooker. The point of the nose almost suggests an arrow being aimed at a target and the target of increased custom was certainly being achieved. No. 43029 has lost its 'W' prefix on the number by this stage of its service, though it has gained the rooftop exhaust cowling that was necessary to reduce the effect of dirty exhaust staining the yellow paint on trailing power cars. Note the parcels 'BRUTES' that were ever present around the ends of station platforms for many years, ready to accept the parcel traffic that BR used to cater for on most of its longer-distance passenger services. *Graham Smith*

Motive Power Matters – The Fame of the Nose

LEFT Mixing it with the rather less appealing designs of AC electric locos 87006 *George Reynolds* and 86224 plus a class 323 EMU, 43159 is caught under the 'new' footbridge at Birmingham's New Street station 1 April 2001. It is on Cross Country duty for Virgin Trains. The open door suggests a crew change or perhaps the driver has popped back to grab a coffee from the buffet, provided the train is not running late, of course. The Virgin West Coast class 87 would presently be propelling its set of coaches southwards as the next departure to London Euston, while the Cross Country-owned class 86 would likely be going the other way in the direction of Manchester. New Street used to rely on its central concourse-level corridor for access to all platforms, an area that would get very congested at times of disruption as people waited for information or queued for refreshments; the 1993-built footbridge seen here helped to relieve that pressure somewhat. It is a pity that the more recent and very expensive rebuild of the station has done little to improve the lot of the passenger who has to change trains here. HST experts will be aware that 43159 (together with 43102) achieved a world record speed for diesel traction of 148.5mph on 1 November 1987 between Northallerton and York, during testing of the SIG bogie intended for use with the incoming mark 4 rolling stock.

LEFT There is nothing especially unusual about this shot but the lighting at Swansea station on 29 July 2005 seems to have illuminated the front end features of 43154 and 43009 rather nicely – it helps that both vehicles are relatively clean. The FGW power car had been one of the first to be fitted with the new 4000 series engine from MTU. After the success of the initial trials, all other power cars that still had the original Paxman Valenta were re-engined with the MTU. While the newer engine was clearly much more efficient than the old, it required pre-heating before use and didn't exactly fit the original engine bay; with sixteen cylinders, as against twelve, it was longer and also slightly wider than the Valenta and wasn't so easy for footplate staff to squeeze past, should they need to during running.

LEFT Parked on the cleaning and fuelling roads at Neville Hill depot, Leeds, on 25 April 2009 is 43072 *Derby Etches Park*. Two years later this power car would be renumbered to 43272, losing its name on transfer to East Coast (when it also had its Paxman VP185 replaced with an MTU engine), only to return to Midland Main Line duties again when the HSTs had finished service on the ECML in 2019! It is carrying the livery of the Midland Mainline TOC with the branding of East Midlands Trains, formed in 2007.

RIGHT If the electrification of the East Coast Main Line had been extended onwards to Aberdeen in 1991, there may well have been little need for any diesel working out of King's Cross. As a result of that omission, the sight of three or four HST sets at this terminus remained a regular occurrence through the Nineties and well into the twenty-first century. Nos 43317, 43251 and 43306 gleam in the afternoon sunshine on 19 May 2009, together with electric 91113, still retaining its GNER dark blue as a small reminder of more prosperous times. By this stage, the East Coast franchise was well into its 'revolving door' phase of whoever was in charge of its services, not helped by a combination of a downturn in custom following the 2008 economic problems and a Department for Transport keeping everyone guessing as to what peculiar decision it might take next! The emergency coupling hatch would sometimes hang slightly open on the power cars, as seen here on 43317, as if suggesting that the train might have its own opinion …

No. 43044 slips out of the holding sidings at Cricklewood and along behind the station platforms, heading in to St Pancras to form one of the evening departures on 21 September 2011. The angle of the house roof in the background practically matches that of the power car's front and I wonder at the variety of motive power that will have been witnessed from those windows over the years. The design of the HST won many accolades: In 1976, the Worshipful Company of Carmen awarded its Viva Shield (for notable contributions to the advancement of transport) to it, stating that it 'represented a stage of technical development in commercial operation second to none in the world'. Two years later, on presenting its award, the Design Council said that it had been 'impressed that so many varied engineering disciplines had come together in a single product of such high overall quality'. And the GRP cab (developed at the RTC in Derby) won an award from the British Plastics Federation. What other train has put so many trophies in the cabinet?

Twin PCs

No. 43196 *Rio Prince* and 43087 *Rio Invader* are paired up in the yard at Etches Park on 17 May 2005, both off lease having completed their short-term careers with MML and now awaiting orders (see subsequent images). Sharp-eyed readers may notice that one power car has the stag logo applied, while the other features the rather non-descript National Express symbol. All these changes make you wonder whether railway managers had the transfer manufacturers on speed dial. But do passengers really care whose symbol is on the side of their train? These sidings were in a relatively quiet period of use at the time, having once been carriage sidings and before that, the site of Derby's steam locomotive shed. A new Meridian DMU servicing facility was shortly to be built here and the tracks remodelled accordingly.

Motive Power Matters – Twin PCs

LEFT This minor face-off at Craigentinny caught my eye, as our team of technicians waited for the operational NMT to be released for service by the depot (using 43014 and 43062). These two spare PCs (for the NMT) are 43013 and 43196, parked on the main-line side of the shed on 9 January 2006. The latter unit had just been taken on in place of 43154, which had been put to one side in the autumn and would soon be forwarded to Landore depot for overhaul and further service with FGW. I never did keep up with what power cars were owned by which leasing company but I suspect there were leasing agreements involved in these exchanges! No. 43196 seemed no different to 43154, after all. The camera housings on the regular NMT power cars did them no favours in their appearance; however, they were fitted for a good reason and being able to view where the train was going from inside the monitoring vehicles was of enormous help to the technicians, not to mention the useful video that was recorded for other Network Rail departments.

RIGHT The red 'Hornby' livery applied to 43087 was perhaps the most notable paint job to be given to an HST power car; what railway enthusiast could possibly object to an advert for the very thing that probably began their interest in railways, when they were young? On 10 February 2006, it is shown crossing over to the down main at Honeybourne, having come along the branch line from Long Marston with its hired partner 43070 (sporting Cotswold Rail silver paint). While not required to haul charter trains for CR, these two have just brought a rake from Tyseley to Long Marston. Almost unknown in BR days was the use of pairs of power cars as a single locomotive; this was something that began to be seen increasingly frequently around this time, for example when the up Penzance sleeper suffered a failure of its rostered class 57. It appears it may become a more regular sight with new operators. *Bob Sweet*

OVERLEAF Brand new out of the Works at Crewe come numbers SC43091 and SC43090 on 1 June 1978. As with several others, these Scottish-allocated examples were initially loaned to Heaton depot, possibly because Craigentinny wasn't yet ready to receive them. At the time of writing exactly forty-three years later the latter is working as a stand-in power car on the NMT (as 43290) while the regular units undergo modification for ETCS operation. *Arthur Turner/Transport Treasury*

The Human Element

A passenger train is nothing without the people who maintain it, operate it and travel on it. Here we feature all of them plus some of the names bestowed on certain power cars to brighten their lives of (hitherto) anonymity.

In the Cab

The driving cab is such a fundamental part of any train that that it deserves to be included in this book. And preferably with somebody in it! Who better to put in the 'best seat in the house' than East Coast driver Mick Barstow? Mick is a well-known enthusiast and photographer himself and is seen here on his very last working shift on Monday, 21 July 2014, after forty years on the railway. Having taken an electric (91110) up to Newcastle in the morning, he returned home on the up 'Highland Chieftain' (1E13 07.55 Inverness to King's Cross) – an HST turn, naturally. Mick's friend, Nick Green, has captured him near Northallerton, relaxed though fully in control as 43239 leads his train southwards at 125mph. His left hand is touching the brake handle, which is in the 'running' position – i.e. not yet applied. *Nick Green*

THE HUMAN ELEMENT – IN THE CAB

LEFT An expertly captured image of the famous speed record sign at Little Bytham, between Grantham and Peterborough. In 1938, it was this racing stretch where *Mallard* was given its head going south downhill from Stoke Summit and briefly attained a world record for steam traction of 126mph. Mick admitted that he was touching that speed himself; his own small tribute at the controls of an HST, surely a very worthy successor to Gresley's streamlined A4 Pacifics. If you are a passenger on an East Coast train hoping to catch a glimpse of the sign (and at 125mph it will only be a glimpse!), you need to look to the eastern (up) side of the track near to milepost 90. Unhelpfully, the mileposts are on the down side. *Nick Green*

The red line is at 125mph, just in case anyone should happen to overlook it and in the early days of the HST, quite a few drivers 'accidentally' did just that. There was no speed limiter or reminder back then to stop them, so the temptation to 'see what she'll do' was too much for some to resist. Officially, 'she' proved capable under test conditions of 148mph with a five-coach load; thank goodness the speedo was calibrated up to 150! Mick informs me that now power would be cut off should the train reach 129mph, but with today's OTMR (On Train Monitoring Recorder, the railway industry's spy-in-the-cab) any driver that kept pushing that would find him or herself with some explaining to do when the information was downloaded for inspection. *Nick Green*

It doesn't look too remarkable but this is the power controller. This offers five notches and normal practice is to get the train under way from a typical stop using one and two, before moving it all the way to five when 15–20mph is reached – given a clear road, of course! Line speed will be reached in minutes, depending on load/gradient/rail conditions etc. Notch three or four would usually be adequate to keep the train rolling at full speed on the level, and there's plenty of that on the East Coast. The big chromed button alongside is the AWS cancelling device; the driver must press this firmly should the train encounter any adverse signals (double yellow, single yellow or red) or speed restrictions. Failure to do so promptly results in the brakes applying and the train coming to a complete (and embarrassing) halt. With authority from the signaller, pressing it also overrides the TPWS should a signal need to be passed at danger. The key on the right is the master switch that allows the driver to activate the controls, once the key has been inserted. *Nick Green*

It's on a Plate

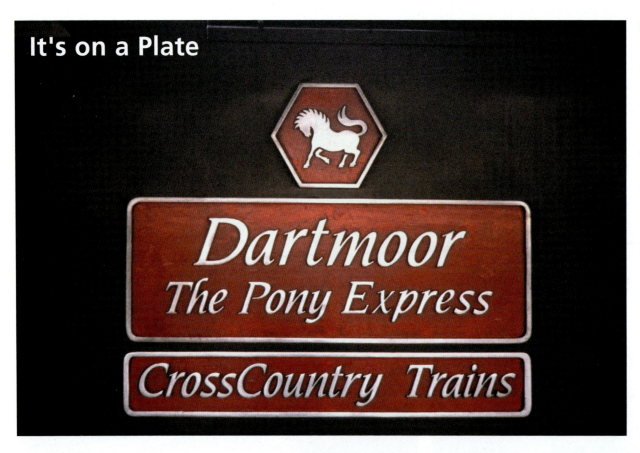

LEFT No. 43158 became *Dartmoor – The Pony Express* at Plymouth station on 12 March 1995, when ten-year-old Ben Doonan did the honours after winning a competition in a local newspaper. The italic style of writing was novel; it seemed that the Cross Country Trains business was anxious to leave its mark on railway history before privatisation set in. A further naming on the same day saw 43193 become *Plymouth Spirit of Discovery* when unveiled by renowned yachtsman Robin Knox-Johnston. These plates on 43158 were seen at Sheffield on 16 October 1996, the *CrossCountry Trains* one no doubt being removed after Virgin took over. *John Tolson/Transport Treasury*

RIGHT The HST arrived at a time when the naming of locomotives was still regarded as something rather anachronistic; it smacked of the steam age and had no place on a forward-looking BR in 1976. That view changed slowly, beginning when the Stephenson Locomotive Society instigated the naming of electric locomotive 87001 *Stephenson* to mark the 150th anniversary of the Stockton & Darlington Railway; other class members followed and the momentum continued. The first HST power car to receive a name was 43113 *City of Newcastle upon Tyne* in 1983. The following year 43057 was named *Bounds Green*, being one of several Eastern Region units to give publicity to the depots that maintained them; *Neville Hill*, *Heaton* and *Craigentinny* were the others. Railwayana like this can sell at auction for thousands of pounds today. This photo was taken at Derby on 15 April 1984, by which being carried on the nose. *Arthur Turner/Transport Treasury*

THE HUMAN ELEMENT – IT'S ON A PLATE

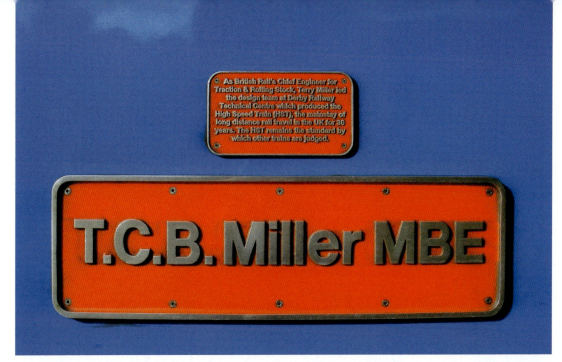

LEFT Sir Kenneth Grange is well known as being the designer of the HST's unmistakable front end, but the train wouldn't have become what it has without the contribution of Terry Miller. Appointed BR's Chief Engineer of Traction and Rolling Stock in 1968, he led the team that devised it as the stopgap alternative to the ground-breaking Advanced Passenger Train. The stopgap then became the back-stop for the rail business when the APT couldn't deliver what it had promised. No. 43048 was named *T.C.B. Miller MBE* on 30 April 2008. The additional plaque talks about the train being the mainstay of long-distance rail travel for thirty years; we are now past forty and still counting, of course. *The standard by which other trains are judged* … what more can be said?

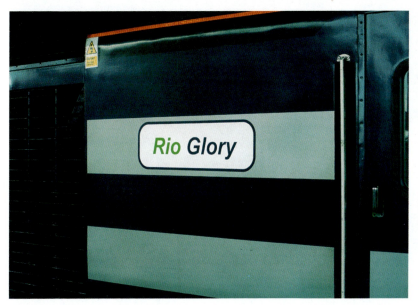

Not exactly a plate, just a transfer this one, on 43180. 'Project Rio' was said to have taken its name from the Manchester United footballer Rio Ferdinand and was drawn up at the request of the erstwhile Strategic Rail Authority, using ex-Virgin Cross Country HSTs that had been well-used and were in clear need of an overhaul; reliability was not so good! Nevertheless, the maintenance team at Derby Etches Park were given a morale boost when permission was granted to apply names in this style. *Rio Glory* was seen at St Pancras on 31 August 2004 before working to Manchester Piccadilly with 43088, to be named *Rio Campaigner* soon after. As for the naming theme, fans of the Western-class diesel-hydraulics need no clues as to where the inspiration came from!

The railway director, Chris Green is likely to be recalled in any account of HST history through his successful tenure with InterCity. As Virgin Trains' Chief Executive, he was present at Paddington on 11 December 2001 when 43102 was named *HST Silver Jubilee* by railway author Colin Marsden, who also presented Chris with a copy of his book of the same name. It was estimated back then that the 196 power cars and 750 trailer vehicles in the fleet had covered more than 500 million miles in service. Would it be too confident a prediction to say that by the time the train's everyday presence on our network is over, that figure will have exceeded one billion? It must have been a proud day for Colin – the other power car present that day (43197 *The Railway Magazine*) he had also named five years before! *Bob Sweet*

Open to the Public

GWR's High Speed Train maintenance facility at St Philip's Marsh staged a sell-out Open Day on 2 May 2016. Not apparent from many of the photos published at the time was that the event was hampered by heavy rain for most of the day. Nevertheless, spirits of the 5,000-plus visitors attending were hardly dampened, given the fantastic array of motive power on display, the principal feature of which was this line-up of HST power cars to mark the type's forty years of service: 43172 *Harry Patch*, 43423, 43013, 43300 *Craigentinny*, 43048 *T.C.B. Miller MBE* and 43187. I've managed to squeeze into the shot the other two stars of the show, the prototype 41001 and 43002 *Sir Kenneth Grange*, not to mention LMS 4-6-0 46100 *Royal Scot* and a smattering of umbrellas queuing for a look inside one of the cabs; the steam loco would probably have been the star attraction at most other displays! Towards closing time, the sun decided to put in a belated appearance, leading to a scramble to get some sunny photos before marching orders were issued.

THE HUMAN ELEMENT – OPEN TO THE PUBLIC

Here comes the sun. And there goes the man himself; ghosting through the hi-viz jackets and anoraks in his frock coat and top hat is Mr Isambard Kingdom Brunel, clearly feeling it was time to see what all the fuss was about. This was one of those moments that you just raise the camera and shoot; if I'd tried to assess the situation in any way, the moment would have passed. I like the other headgear on display too – those youngsters' matching caps and the bump cap in the foreground that is clearly a tribute to the Grand Central livery! Some of the depot was fenced off from visitors to maintain operations during the day. Under today's health and safety conditions, it is no small feat to put on any event like this but the figure of over £20,000 raised for local charity 'Springboard Opportunity Group' (that helps children with special needs) clearly made the effort worthwhile.

On the very next day, courtesy of our friends in the Rail Operations Group, some of the event's exhibits returned north as 5Z43 06.29 St Philip's Marsh–Derby Etches Park. The convoy is seen passing Lea Marston, top and tailed by 43300 and 43048 (which was also powered up). No. 41001 and three of the coaches owned by the 125 Group were being returned to Ruddington at the Great Central Railway (Nottingham), when the prototype power car was on loan from the National Railway Museum. Two of these coaches have since been changed for others, as the Group has sought to assemble an authentic rake of vehicles making up an eight-coach train. Compared with other preservation groups that have perhaps only had a single locomotive to worry about, the 125 Group have set themselves a considerable task in seeking to obtain a wide range of typical rolling stock and equipment from the HST's long history. *Jason Rogers*

No. 43002 *Sir Kenneth Grange* has since found a home at the NRM too. Here it is with the replica of *Rocket*, the two engines almost book-ending the motive power of Britain's railways. What else might they have in common, other than the width between their wheels? Well, both had a great impact on the public in their day. With the small matter of a century and a half separating them, of course.

Passengers and Professionals

LEFT Let's do this. There is something of that look on the face of the driver of 43022 as he brings his Paddington–Penzance train into Exeter St David's on 20 July 1982. But is it one of resignation or determination? His cap may not be too straight but is he secretly glad to be back doing what he loves; who can tell? The previous day, the country's train drivers had returned to work after a two-week strike over flexible rostering. It was one of those concepts of which the travelling public at first knew nothing, though soon came to be experts upon. The drivers' union ASLEF had wanted to stick to the traditional eight-hour working day. However, British Rail, unable to negotiate the changes they sought, had imposed a variable seven-to-nine-hour working day, which led to a strike commencing on 4 July. With an apparent lack of support from the leader of the NUR (the railwaymen's union), matters came to a head when BR threatened to sack any driver who wouldn't accept the new arrangement and return to work. Double manning (as seen here) was to remain for a while, at least. Semaphores, 'Peak' class 45143 *5th Royal Inniskilling Dragoon Guards* and a class 08 'Gronk' complete the typical scene of that period. *Arthur Turner/Transport Treasury*

RIGHT For this train conductor, clutching his trusty T-key in his left hand, he's having to move down the train quickly without getting too wet in the process – perhaps walking from his compartment in TGS 44033 through the train itself would take too long, as time is pressing. No. 43018 in original FGW livery is at the rear of this Swansea–Paddington service at Newport on 9 July 2004. A class 60 is in evidence at the Godfrey Road stabling point, one of the dwindling number of locations in South Wales where locomotives could be seen gathered between their freight duties.

Carlisle has long been one of the great railway crossroads of the country. However, it did not witness regular visits from HSTs until the 1990s. Until then, those that worked cross-country into Scotland largely did so via the East Coast Main Line, leaving West Coast-routed workings to be formed of locomotive-hauled coaching stock (with a switch to or from electric haulage in the Midlands). Pictured is the 07.25 Plymouth–Aberdeen, as it glides into platform 3 with a varied assembly of passengers waiting to board; you can tell it's a Saturday – there is only casual dress on display. The date is 14 August 1993 and the deposits in the four foot (despite those entreaties *not* to flush in the station) serve as a reminder that a weakness of the mark 3 design was the lack of waste retention tanks. That was to become more of an issue as the HST's length of service progressed.

Come on, I know you're in there. The emergency coupling bar of 43087 is being coaxed out by one of the Maintrain staff at Derby station in readiness for it to be hauled into the sidings at Etches Park by 08899. Both it and 43196 had been in store since the ending of the 'Rio' services and were about to be prepared for employment on extra summer trains to the South West. The instruction to 'MML Drivers' on the cab side of the shunter is interesting; it's a pity the wording can't be read but clearly the manager who wrote it felt it was too important to be left for the signing-on noticeboard. Witness also the taped message on the windscreen of 43087 – 'Do not start the engine'? On 10 May 2005, the former Midland Railway offices building in the background was empty but would soon be taken on by Derby College as a campus, reopening it in 2009.

RIGHT Having not gone west of Plymouth for most of its early deployment, changes to the operating schedule of the NMT in 2014 saw Penzance being reached every four weeks. On 11 April, 43014 provides the backdrop for a conversation piece involving three enthusiasts who would appear to be considering their next move. Whatever it was, there would be no hurry to decide at this relatively quiet western outpost of the railway system. Perhaps a walk across to St Michael's Mount in the background is out of the question, however on this pleasantly sunny day – too wet. 'Authorised Personnel Only' reads the notice on the door to the driver's cab; would anyone inclined to read that actually need to be so informed?

LEFT That's what it's there for. The long-handled brush is deployed to wash the headlights on 43154 at Plymouth on 2 September 2005. Serco driver Gary Payne will shortly be taking the NMT back to London on the return leg of its early morning monitoring run from Old Oak Common. Accompanied by 43067 at the other end, the use of the two temporarily hired power cars meant that no video of the line would be recorded on this occasion; the expense of equipping them with cameras for the sake of a few months service with Network Rail couldn't be justified but the all-over yellow livery was clearly a must. In 2021, when power cars were borrowed for NMT use once again, the long-standing 'all-yellow' stipulation for the train's livery had sadly been dropped!

LEFT What do you reckon? A GWR employee at Totnes station has for some reason felt the need to walk down the end of the platform and speak directly to the driver of a Cross Country service on 13 September 2018. He is clutching a despatch bat; this comes in handy on a platform thronged with passengers when the 'right away' signal needs to be given clearly to the guard, instead of just the normal raised arm. No. 43378 is being held in the platform while another westbound service gets priority to proceed over Rattery Incline, which begins almost from the platform end.

FACING PAGE You can still enjoy scenic Scottish train rides all day in the comfort of an HST, of course. On 18 May 2021, 43031 brings 1H07 08.35 Edinburgh Waverley–Inverness into Aviemore as a southbound class 170 awaits its arrival in the station loop. A quick word with the DMU's driver on the left revealed that, while he also signed class 43s, he still preferred the newer traction!

RIGHT In complete contrast to the image taken at Newport, this train's conductor appears somewhat more relaxed, though you still get the impression she may have an errant passenger or two in her sights. These members of railway staff experience the full range of human interaction in their job, from helping happy travellers on their holidays to dealing with late-night drunks who don't have a ticket. The setting is Edinburgh Waverley on 20 April 2016 and 43302 is at the head of Virgin Trains East Coast's 1S03 07.10 Leeds–Aberdeen service. This station could hardly be better placed to serve the city of Edinburgh, certainly from a tourist's point of view, as so many of its attractions are within walking distance from it. Consequently rail travel holds its own against the speed of internal air services, which are always handicapped by their airports being out of town. And besides, why would you want to miss out on the scenery offered by the rail journey? *Keith Sanders*

Colourful HSTs

And so to perhaps the most colourful years of the High Speed Train. Privatisation let loose all the colours of the rainbow as the new train operating companies sought to get their trains into the limelight. Which ones were the most successful? Was it the classic and the corporate, the radical or just simply red? On those questions, the jury may be out for some time yet!

Blue is the Colour

… and High Speed is the Train? Not for this late-morning departure about to be made from Manchester Piccadilly station on 7 April 2004; the brakes seemed to be reluctant to let go as the driver of 43071 applied the power! All was well eventually, however, and 43196 would soon trail this formation dutifully towards Stockport and the Hope Valley route to Derby. The purpose of these temporary services under 'Project Rio' was to provide an alternative route to London, even though some Virgin Pendolino trains were still clearly running. Quite why it was necessary to apply the capital R in front of the number of the power cars used was a mystery. In practice, they were sometimes employed on regular St Pancras route services. The Rio names that these power cars received were at the initiative of the engineering department and only for the final two weeks that these trains ran in August-September 2004. No. 43071 escaped the privilege through being unavailable for service at the time.

Colourful HSTs – Blue is the Colour

At Hasland, south of Chesterfield, we find 43047 leading the 15.25 from Sheffield to St Pancras, with 43166 doing the honours at the rear on 11 April 2007. The more you study this livery, the more you get the feel that it was a throwback to British Rail; an essentially blue locomotive pulling a rake of blue and grey coaches. Following the eye-catching display of the previous design, it must count as a disappointment. The slow lines here were still alive with coal trains in 2007 and Freightliner's 66554 can be glimpsed behind on a Hull–Rugeley Power Station duty. The latter installation was in the process of being demolished at the time of writing and this was expected to be complete by the end of 2021. As for 43047, it had begun life as part of the first tranche of HSTs ordered for the Western Region in 1976. During the 1980s, a reshuffling of services in the InterCity sector brought it onto the Midland Main Line and it became one of the first recipients of the Paxman VP185 power unit in 1995.

LEFT A close-up look at a central portion of 42573 (ex-41127) at Kingham station on the Cotswold line. FGW seemed to be the only operator choosing to place the coach numbers centrally on the bodyside. This also shows how the window edges of a train become susceptible to damage and then inevitably rust. Modifications under FGW that rather spoiled the travel experience for passengers were the almost total removal of seats around tables in standard class together with the fitment of seats with very high backs, as shown here; if you had an aisle seat, then that was pretty much all you would see. One of the arguments for having these was that, in the event of a severe derailment, they would prevent passengers from being thrown around inside the vehicle. A rejoinder to that might be, how often does that actually happen and shouldn't the industry be concentrating its resources on preventing derailments in the first place? For the writer, one of the joys of rail travel is the view out of the window and it seems that high seat backs only encourage people to look at their mobile phones – as if they don't do quite enough of that already!

LEFT Up to line speed after the Swindon stop, 43028 heads 1A15, the 11.30 Bristol Temple Meads to London Paddington, on 19 April 2018. Having been part of set 253014 when it was new in August 1976, the power car had been covering this journey throughout an incredible forty-two years of service before being transferred to Scotrail's Haymarket depot. Improvements to the track on this section of line to permit higher-speed running began back in 1972, with uniformly deep ballast being laid and some track realignment in places. Electrification in the twenty-first century presented a new set of challenges. In 2014, in conjunction with the *Architects' Journal*, *Rail Engineer* magazine launched a competition for 'new, aesthetically pleasing designs for the gantry and cantilever structures on the UK rail network which could play a part in the way Britain's railway implement future electrification schemes' – sadly too late for the Great Western scheme, which in places looks like an upset box of Meccano.

BELOW It's 19 April 2018 and HSTs are now sharing the workload over the Great Western Main Line, roughly half and half with the burgeoning fleet of class 800s. The proportion was shifting all the time in the latter's favour as these Hitachi-designed trains came off the production (assembly?) line at Heighington in County Durham. This photo is an attempt at getting deliberate speed blur in an image. Using 1/80 second shutter speed, the camera is held as steadily as possible before trying to avoid jabbing at the button as the right moment to shoot approaches. Let's be honest and say that there's a fair amount of luck involved with this; if the nose of the power car had made it to the edge of the frame, I probably would have deleted the shot there and then. I decided to include the brambles, partly to create a natural foreground to counterbalance the concrete of the bridge and barrier. Ashbury Crossing, near Shrivenham, is a popular place to observe traffic between Didcot and Swindon. When the HSTs were first introduced in the Seventies, a quiet level crossing was closed here and the bridge erected to allow walkers, cyclists and horse riders to cross the track in complete safety.

Colourful HSTs – Blue is the Colour

LEFT With trains being diverted from the Great Western Main Line via the Greenford loop and Bicester's Gavray Curve, 43192 passes through High Wycombe at the rear of a train bound for Paddington on 7 May 2018. Up front was number 43063. This station was, of course, frequented by the HST's spiritual predecessor the Blue Pullman, which ran non-stop between Paddington and Wolverhampton Low Level from 1960 to 1966. It is remarkable to consider how, within the space of fewer than fifteen years, technological progress could be made from using power cars that had 1,000hp engines to ones that packed 2,250hp each. The Pullmans would have mostly used the centre roads here, which were removed with the Marylebone area resignalling scheme of 1990.

ABOVE So what exactly was wrong with this livery? The 'dynamic' lines might have been a little fussy but overall this wasn't a bad colour scheme. Unfortunately, the decision was subsequently taken to standardise with an overall dark blue, just keeping the waving lines on the coaches and thus almost repeating the error that was made with the second Midland Mainline livery – the HST is best treated as a complete entity and not as a locomotive and coaches arrangement. No. 43004 *First for the future/First ar gyfer y dyfodol* is shown at Newton Abbot on 3 April 2006, the day that a demonstration run was made as the 09.12 from Paddington to Penzance, via Bristol. With 43009 *First transforming travel* (no Welsh translation!) bringing up the rear of a short-formed set, this proved to be a one-off display. *Bob Sweet*

Ladies in Red

One of the early franchises awarded in the newly privatised railway was perhaps bound to choose red as the basis of their livery. The Virgin Group had red airliners, so red trains were likely to follow! Their livery was launched with a special train on 6 January 1997 featuring power cars 43063 and 43068, though the train had staged something of a curtain-raiser beforehand when it was tested on the 3rd and filmed traversing the snowy Settle and Carlisle route on the 4th. With a nod towards what was to come, 43063 received the name *Maiden Voyager* at the launch in Edinburgh before working the 'Cornish Scot' to Penzance. On 3 February, 43093 was named *Lady in Red* when it ran between Manchester and Bournemouth as the 'Pines Express', in company with 43063. On 10 July 1997, 43063 cruises through the curves at Beckfoot (with 43067) as the 08.50 Edinburgh–Penzance 'Cornish Scot'; notice the larger than normal cab-side numbers and frontal yellow extended over the cab roof. *Bill Atkinson*

RIGHT The infrastructure around Burton upon Trent points to a more active railway past than exists today, not least because of the internal railway network that served the many breweries characterising the town. The Bonded Warehouse in the background was built by the Midland Railway as a malting for the brewing industry and its metre-thick walls are highly suitable for the wine storage role performed today. Sadly, the industry that remains does not use rail transport to the extent of former days. The several bridge arches and vacant ground to the side of the main line suggest that more tracks once ran here, as 43014 leads a NE–SW service towards the station on 16 July 2001; 43099 was the rear power car. No. 43014 would be taken on by Network Rail little more than a year later for use with the New Measurement Train.

LEFT The privatised railway is here, though the hardware on display at Crewe on 10 June 2000 is very much that of British Rail. No. 43158 (and 43090) form the 11.20 Glasgow–Penzance, pulling away from platform 5 while a class 47 has responsibility for the 10.40 Edinburgh–Brighton at platform 6. The smoky exhaust from an HST's Paxman engine was a familiar sight, especially following twenty-odd years of intensive service, and it was becoming clear to operators that a new power unit would be required for all of them if they were to continue in the leading role to which they'd been accustomed. No. 43158 had apparently (at least on one side) lost the nameplates it had received only five years before. A reversion to a black-painted cab roof is clear plus the 'XC' addition to the Virgin logo is also dispensed with. It is interesting how the through lines at Crewe station are laid with wooden sleepers, reducing weight on the service tunnels beneath presumably, while there is a ruling speed restriction of 80mph.

Virgin Trains were in two minds as to whether they would keep any of their HST sets upon the roll-out of their much anticipated 'Operation Princess' in 2002. A few five-coach sets were retained as a 'Challenger' fleet to supplement the new Voyager DMUs, with a view to using them on certain newly formulated services. This came to nought and just prior to their decision not to proceed with that plan, 43086 is captured rounding the curve at Heamies Farm, Norton Bridge. No. 43196 (another one to later serve briefly with the NMT) was running at the rear of a rake of vehicles that appear to have all had recent attention to their coil springs, as they head towards Birmingham New Street on 22 March 2003. VT had been forced to run HSTs even shorter than this late in 2000 following a spate of axlebox problems that were unexpectedly brought on by water ingress.

No. 43068 was named *The Red Nose* at London Paddington on 3 March 1997 during a spell when the Virgin publicity machine was clearly in overdrive. But by the time of this photo at Rugeley Trent Valley on 25 September 2003, it was carrying *The Red Arrows* name on its side, one that had previously been applied to 43155! The first of the buffer-fitted power cars, 43123 was bringing up the rear of this Manchester Piccadilly–Euston service. It would appear that around this period it was possible to travel between London and Manchester on an HST set over two different routes!

Mix and Match

Say 'Lickey Bank' to a railway enthusiast and he or she will know exactly where you mean. Perhaps if you say 'Vigo' then only a local one will know that it's a place just below the top of the incline where it's always been the best spot to witness motive power pushed to its limit. As far as passenger trains are concerned, the coming of the High Speed Train (with its high power-to-weight ratio) was the first time that this obstacle could truly be said to have been tamed. But only if both power cars were working, of course! On 23 September 1998, the 08.21 Paignton–Newcastle toils up the grade with 43160 and 43155 doing the honours, both in Virgin livery but sandwiching InterCity stock. A fully functioning set would normally be maintaining a steady 70mph by this point; passengers would hardly notice the reduction in speed, partly because there was always a limit of 80 or 90 anyway through Bromsgrove station, at the foot of the climb.

Colourful HSTs – Mix and Match

The fag packet livery is on borrowed time on 20 April 2002, as 43142 parades the First Group colours at Aller – first attempt! Only some of the FGW fleet were turned out in this style before the decision was taken to drop the white element and replace it with more blue; by the following year, the HST repaints had been completed but the class 180s kept their white. Sadly, this long-standing and popular vantage point for train observers (just outside Newton Abbot) is no more, due to the demolition of the farmer's access bridge over the railway here and the widening of the extremely busy A380 road in the background. The milepost on the left states '215', which is the mileage from London Paddington via Bath and Bristol; this is approximately 20 miles longer than the route that this train would have followed via the Berks & Hants.

ABOVE At a time when all manner of liveries seemed to be playing out among the Midland Mainline fleet, ex-Virgin 43193 has been pressed into use on a Sheffield–St Pancras working passing Chevinside (north of Derby) on 29 May 2003, with a more familiar 43051 at the rear. It still retains its *Plymouth Spirit of Discovery* (painted with a very obvious white background) and *CrossCountry Trains* plates that were affixed in March 1995. During a relatively short spell with MML, it acquired *Rio Triumph* transfer nameplates before spending the rest of its operational career on Great Western. At the time of writing, it is in storage at Long Marston with a most uncertain future ahead of it.

RIGHT Upon the magnificent frontage of Nottingham station, British Rail's double arrow symbol still flies approximately fourteen years after privatisation. The reduction in the number of tracks at the station's west end and the establishment of a staff car park has provided a view of trains with a nice backdrop that wasn't possible previously; usually it seems to be a case of good spots being lost. On 6 March 2009, 43083 sports the full East Midlands Trains livery departing as the 15.27 to St Pancras, while the coaches do that in name only.

Somewhat overshadowed by its Hornby-liveried playing partner under the Cotswold Rail banner, number 43070 was given quite a striking all-over silver paint job. As has become fashionable, the company's website address was stated very clearly on its bodyside, presumably in case anyone seeing it might have been unaware of the company's existence and wanted further information. Coaches remained in the livery of Midland Mainline, their previous operator. The set was kept at Tyseley depot in Birmingham while work could be found for it, but it is seen on 10 February 2006 leaving the single-line section from Norton Junction en route to Long Marston, one of the country's favoured sites for storage of rolling stock, pending further activity. The 'plywood wonder' signal box here at Evesham has 'W.R.' appended to its nameboard, which harks back to the days when the town had separate (though adjacent) stations for Western and London Midland Region services; only the former remains.

NMT - How the Test is Done

Let's start with a close look at the business end of the New Measurement Train. This shows 43062 in Etches Park sidings, Derby, on 9 May 2003. With 43013, the set was about to conduct braking trials between Darlington and York as one of its first outings on the network. The wording shown here was not the first attempt, however; since February, this unit and 43013 had been displaying the wording *I³ Integrated Infrastructure Inspection* instead of *Head of Examination Chief Engineers Dept*. Whoever came up with the first suggestion I don't know, but it obviously didn't sit well with the powers-that-be and so it was changed. Along with other earlier-built power cars, the guard's compartment window would be removed and blanked off during refurbishment. I recall seeing a handset still perched on a ledge in one corner, a leftover from when guards were expected to sit there if not attending to passengers. I'm not surprised they objected to this and demanded their own place in the adjoining coaches; it was a grubby, noisy, draughty and uncomfortable place to be at high speed.

ABOVE No. 43062 waits to leave the bay at Darlington during the braking trials on 10 May 2003. The two power cars had been idling for quite a while before they left Derby the first time. When the driver opened the throttle, the somewhat tired Valenta diesels promptly covered the northern outskirts of the town with thick fumes. It might not be obvious at first glance but the shade of yellow painted centrally on the front was slightly different to that on the side of the train! Keeping a uniform shade of the colour across the vehicles proved difficult to maintain as one by one they visited the shops for attention. The most obvious modification at the front, though, is obviously the camera housing. At this stage the screen wipers had yet to be fitted and, based upon those employed for building security, they didn't take kindly to being asked to function at 2 miles per minute. During test runs at Old Dalby, a dozy pheasant unwillingly decided to enter one box, narrowly missing the camera.

RIGHT It's hard to resist including this coach view as it was parked briefly in front of the Network Rail training facility at Bristol Parkway on 11 April 2014. On several occasions, Conference Coach 975814 was itself used as a training facility for budding permanent way engineers and other interested rail staff, not to mention the on-train monitoring technicians (of whom I was one). A large presentation screen at one end of the saloon overlooked a table around which twelve people could sit, and this was the perfect 'on-location' classroom to have for any railway presentation. Not all the set's vehicles were fitted with steps underneath each door to permit easy access from track level.

A year on from the previous photo, the low sunlight shows up the differences in paint shades, as well as inconsistent markings! No. 43062 received its *John Armitt* name in a ceremony at Euston on 16 July 2007 after the CEO of Network Rail, who was approaching retirement. Note the airflow testing probe protruding from the front; one working shift was lost when this was first fitted as no official brief had been given to the driver as to what it was for. Quite rightly, he failed the train. Driver Mike Jones is in charge here at Cow Roast, south of Tring, as the train monitors the WCML slow lines in and out of Euston on a warm summer's evening on 9 June 2015.

Colourful HSTs – NMT - How the Test is Done

No lining or logos are to be seen on 43014 as it heads 1Q13 11.40 Heaton Depot to Derby RTC at Settle Junction on 23 July 2012. After spells of being based at Etches Park (Derby) and then Craigentinny (Edinburgh), the NMT has returned to Heaton Depot in Newcastle for its routine weekend servicing since 2007. Monitoring equipment maintenance must still be carried out during visits to the RTC. No. 43014 was later to be (appropriately) named *The Railway Observer* on 14 June 2014, after the journal of the Railway Correspondence & Travel Society. Contrast the condition of the track on the Settle & Carlisle route with that on the 'Little North Western' to the left. Much investment was necessary in the former when it became a preferred way of delivering coal from Scotland to power stations in England; thousands of decades-old wooden sleepers gave way to steel ones carrying welded rail and the NMT was specially re-diagrammed at one stage to monitor its condition.

Stenning's Stunners

National Express were unexpectedly awarded the MML franchise in 1996 and Ray Stenning of the design house *Best Impressions* found himself tasked with creating a fresh look for High Speed Trains. He sought to recall the aura of the great American streamliners of the 1940s and '50s, though with a set of colours that would accommodate that in a forward-looking brand. Those stripes rising from the front had, of course, been seen previously on the LMS Coronation Pacifics, as well as English Electric's prototype 'Deltic' diesel. The colour choice of tangerine and teal was thought by railway managers to be too radical; they needn't have worried as passengers said they preferred it to an alternative darker style that had been proposed. It was described as 'combining the strength and character of the old railway with the vibrancy and modernity of the new'. Seen at St Pancras on 24 May 2002, the stag emblem (perhaps a nod to Sherwood Forest?) is prominent and facing forward on 43075; although this featured on the subsequent MML livery for a time, it was sometimes smaller and facing backwards! Adtranz at the Derby Litchurch Lane Works refurbished the coaches while Neville Hill depot repainted the power cars. Very much of its time, a fax machine was installed in the buffet cars for the use of 'business customers'.

At Chevinside, north of Derby, 43051 heads a Sheffield train away from Milford Tunnel on the bright morning of 15 May 2003, assisted by 43082. The yellow warning area has been cleverly shaped to help give the front a more purposeful look, instead of seeming like an afterthought, though not extended across the cab roof where it would get blackened by the exhaust. Ray Stenning aimed to work with the architecture of Kenneth Grange's design such that his livery would enhance it and vice versa. According to Ray, a train like the HST is four dimensional: apart from its length, height and width there is also its motion. If a train seems raring to go when it is actually stood still, that would suggest that the livery design has performed as intended.

We wind the clock on now to 7 May 2009 and another new owner has called for a radical new livery. Stagecoach were already in control of South West Trains, so this time, when they were put in charge of the Midland route as East Midlands Trains, the colours were already a given. For *Best Impressions* it was a question of how an existing livery should be applied to the HST. However, the off-white element of what was quite acceptable to use on a clean-running electric multiple unit was less applicable to a diesel unit that had form for throwing oil over itself under stress! No. 43058 waits at the rear of a northbound working at Leicester station, its presence apparently echoed by the city centre's Premier Inn tower block behind.

Colourful HSTs – Stenning's Stunners

LEFT At this location of Milton Ernest, preparation has begun for electrification northwards from Bedford with the cutting back of vegetation that temporarily facilitates railway photography; return here today and you will see the full array of ironmongery and an accompanying palisade fence. The driver of 43054 will likely have his power controller in position five now that his train has begun to dig into the climb to Sharnbrook and this should hardly affect his cruising speed at or around 100mph all the way up. Compare that with the experience of drivers of 'Peak'-class diesels in the past, who would watch the speedo needle fall from 90 to 60, and before them, those on a 'Royal Scot' 4-6-0, who would be pegged back even more than that. The train pictured was 1D47, the 15.15 St Pancras International to Nottingham service on 19 March 2018, and this illustrates how heavy service dirt does not show too badly against the base blue on the power car.

RIGHT In the Millhouses district of Sheffield, 43073 accelerates away from the station call just as an example of the new pretender, an incoming 'Meridian' DMU, slows down for the impending yellow signal. It will be observed that the off-white comes right to the front of the DMU, whereas blue is the order of the day for the power car of the HST. With the blue band along the underside of the coaches, this still follows through to produce a 'whole train' look – a single entity, rather than the distinct locomotive and coaches appearance of the previous MML livery. The track to the right is Heeley Loop. The southern approach to Sheffield from Dore was once four tracks, including a dive under nearing the station itself, the location of which can still just be determined from the station carriage wash head shunt at one end and the remnants of old lineside fencing at the other. 10 April 2016.

ABOVE The end of the Stagecoach/Virgin franchise did not see the end of their bright red livery. As before, the government-run operation was in no particular hurry to introduce its own colours in place of the former incumbent's. Livery designers themselves are rarely happy to see their handiwork partly obliterated by advertising. However, this example (marking the centenary of Craigentinny depot) has been done sympathetically and surely constitutes a worthy modification, bearing in mind the long association that 'EC' has had with the High Speed Train. No. 43300 *Craigentinny* rushes past Spittal, south of Berwick, with 1E11 07.52 Aberdeen–London King's Cross on 21 June 2019. *Keith Sanders*

LEFT On 10 May 2018, clumps of gorse at Houndwood, County Durham, bring some colour to the landscape as 43317 heads south leading 1E16, the 13.00 Edinburgh–London King's Cross. The young cattle in the field behind seem to have been startled by the passage of this train, so I wonder whether the driver had just sounded his horn – after all, trains would pass that field many times a day! Stagecoach (with Virgin Trains) turned to Ray Stenning once more in 2015 for their new East Coast livery. As before, the design had to be drawn up in a hurry in order to have two complete trains (albeit electric '225' sets) ready for the franchise launch that was only weeks away. Whatever was produced would need to be translated to suit an HST afterwards. The intention was to feature the colour red quite strongly, in tune with the Virgin brand and somewhat in contrast to its minimal appearance in the previous West Coast franchise's Pendolinos and Voyagers. Note the directional 'switch' of the red waves at the catering vehicle. *Ben Wheeler*

On the first day of June in 2017, 43295 and 43313 rest 'on the blocks' at King's Cross, though in practice trains do not run up to the buffers at terminus stations like this anymore for safety reasons. Everybody likes to see a train fresh out of the workshops with gleaming paint but livery designers have to bear in mind that it soon gets grubby in service; a trip through the automatic washing plant won't necessarily restore the original shine, so a successful livery must still stand out, in spite of the grime. QED?

Look North

After BR's Western Region, it was then the turn of the East Coast Main Line to receive most of the other trains off the production line and the north of the country then became frequented by HSTs. Britain's northernmost city, Inverness still plays host to them on a daily basis.

Bridges of Size

A very long lens is used to pick out 43238 as it heads 1S22 from King's Cross to Stirling on 9 May 2019. This less commonly used viewpoint shows the Royal Tweed and Berwick road bridges beyond the railway. While the river water seems calm enough, the North Sea is sending some breakers in towards Tweedmouth in the distance, where the railway can also be picked out having completed its wide arc above the southern side of the town. The electrification of the ECML has hardly impacted the look of this edifice, thanks to some special planning and design of the support structures. While the River Tweed does mark the boundary between England and Scotland for a fair distance, around Berwick the town and both banks of the river are definitely part of English soil. The railway itself crosses the border about 3 miles north from here. The *National Railway Museum, 40 Years 1975-2015* nameplate plus bodyside branding (no half measures!) were unveiled on this power car on 23 September 2015. It had previously carried the name *National Railway Museum, the First Ten Years* from 1985 and then *City of Dundee* during the days of GNER. *Keith Sanders*

So just what is the best photo to take of the Forth Bridge with a train crossing it? I don't think that is something that railway photographers might agree on, probably as each would have their own tastes and priorities. The bridge is the star of the image, naturally, but the complexity of its girders can too easily hide whatever train might be passing over it. At the time of this photo, I had chosen to stay a couple of nights at the Hawes Inn, which is situated almost directly under the southern approach spans of the bridge. Sleep wasn't to be the best I'd had – trains kept me awake, believe it or not – but the Scottish weather was quite kind and a river trip from the Hawes Pier in Queensferry was most enjoyable. Frustratingly, from the boat the only trains I saw crossing the bridge were some Scotrail DMUs, so I had to resign myself to grabbing this foreshore view of an HST in the evening. On 16 June 2017, the new Queensferry road bridge was just weeks away from its opening, whereupon it would assume the responsibility for the carriage of most of the road traffic over the Forth. The 1964-built bridge had shown premature signs of decay in its suspension wires and was being relegated to carrying buses, cyclists and walkers. Meanwhile, the railway bridge just keeps repaying the investment that was made in it back in 1890 … with just the odd new coat of paint, of course.

ABOVE If you Google 'Tay Bridge', the first suggestion coming back features the word 'disaster'. This is a pity because the current Tay railway bridge (completed seven and a half years after the failure of the original) has served as well as the Forth Bridge, only not in such a dramatic style. On 16 May 2018, the photographer has captured a Virgin East Coast liveried set leaving the city of Dundee in its wake and affording its passengers an impressive view of the 'silvery Tay' (to quote from that infamous poem about the disaster by William Topaz McGonagall!). *Ian Lothian*

LEFT Presence of the all-yellow NMT on 16 July 2010 provides a colourful contrast with the pink paintwork on Tay Bridge South signal box (all-brick constructed to withstand the weather) and the flourishing rosebay willowherb plants, so often seen on Scottish railway cutting sides in summer. No. 43014 leads, while 43013 trails. Data recorded by the train from this stretch will be of particular interest: The track engineer will want to ensure that gauge is consistent across the bridge; any sign that it isn't might point to failing timber bearers, which are critical when you consider there is no ballast on the bridge to help retain the track. Coming off the bridge, the track gauge will widen slightly, as it would be expected to on tighter curves such as these, as long as it's within critical limits. And the weed growth should be evident from the video recorded by the front camera! In Dundee itself, we can see Cox's Stack – an 85m-high chimney that is a remnant of the city's jute industry while further to the right on a hill stands the Dundee Law Beacon memorial, now featured on the sides of Scotrail's HST power cars. *Keith Sanders*

The 17.27 Inverness to Glasgow Queen St, reporting number 1T62, crosses the Findhorn Viaduct at Tomatin on 15 May 2021. With reduced patronage during the Coronavirus pandemic, the four-coach formations of Scotrail's HST sets seem to have been adequate to handle the numbers of passengers on offer; it remains to be seen when the intended five-coach sets will come into use. Road traffic on the parallel A9 (seen in the background and on which vastly more expenditure has been made) is easily overhauled by the trains but time is then lost by them at crossing points on this largely single-track route. If the road is to be dualled throughout, as is proposed, then the railway requires similar enhancement.

Eastern Promises

LEFT GNER (owned by the Sea Containers Group) won the franchise to operate long-distance ECML services in 1996 but chose not to roll out their new livery until the following year. Despite investing heavily in refurbished stock and customer service, a run of bad luck with high-speed derailments affected the business and the short franchise length gave it little chance to recover. A succession of failed franchises would follow as over-optimistic forecasts were tripped up by downturns in the national economy, however slight. An unidentified pair of power cars in the new dark blue livery work a complete rake of IC-liveried stock at Houndwood, going south to London on 29 March 1997. Above the windscreen, the NRN aerial breaks the orange cantrail stripe, applied as a guide to staff as to what level they must keep below in order to be a safe distance from the overhead wires. The colour of the GNER lettering changed from white to gold fairly soon after. The writer recalls making journeys from Newark to Edinburgh on the first train north; despite wearing work clothing and holding a second-class ticket, he was always welcomed into the first-class section in order to enjoy the legendary cooked breakfast. *Keith Sanders*

RIGHT The railway safety authorities' attitude towards the importance of front-end yellow warning panels has gradually shifted. By the time that Grand Central introduced their open access services from Sunderland in 2007, only a small panel (rather reminiscent of those first seen in the early 1960s) was deemed sufficient to satisfy standards. The effectiveness of headlights has become the key factor instead, until the industry gets to a state of allowing nobody on track anywhere while trains are running. Forming the 16.50 'Zephyr' service to Sunderland, 43080 departs from King's Cross on the afternoon of 19 May 2009 and leaves in its wake a much brighter and more visible 43251 in its National Express livery. The presence of open access operators on the ECML has been seen as a thorn in the side of the franchised operator; National Express proved no more successful than GNER. Strangely, no parallel situation was permitted on the West Coast!

But enough of franchises; let's simply study the star of the show. No. 43314 sweeps through the quiet Scottish town of Prestonpans, en route from Edinburgh Waverley to London King's Cross on 7 March 2011. The most obvious front-end alteration to the HST resulted from the reworking of the headlights to an arrangement that was more robust than the original design; lights were also much more effective than before. Those illustrated here combined red tail lamps in the outer pod of each pair, whereas Porterbrook-owned vehicles running for EMT kept these separate in the inner pod of three lights. This nine-coach HST fits nicely underneath the frame of an interesting station footbridge. *Keith Sanders*

No. 43257 follows its train into Leeds station at Whitehall Junction on 25 August 2010. The six bi-directional tracks into the station are marked out very clearly with their respective letters; a potentially confusing array of signals among the overhead wires makes it vital that drivers know which line they are taking and therefore which ones apply to them. On this warm summer's day, the sunblind in the rear cab has been drawn down fully to prevent the cab from heating up too much and overburdening the air con. The train is still carrying National Express colours but with 'East Coast' branding, demonstrating that the franchise is now with the government-sponsored Directly Operated Railways, specifically its East Coast Main Line Company.

RIGHT On 28 December 2016, it's barely mid-afternoon but the sun is already providing its last burst of strong light to illuminate 43480 at the head of a down Grand Central flyer at Frinkley Lane crossing, between Grantham and Newark. With their shorter formations and limited stop schedules, these GC sets must have put in quite a few fast runs on the ECML when given a clear road. My own journey plans never quite coincided with any of their services, unfortunately.

LEFT In 2015, a consortium of Stagecoach and Virgin was awarded the ECML franchise, a situation that to the uninitiated spectator appeared to show that both principal routes between London and Scotland were under the control of Richard Branson. Not so. In spite of appearances, it was Stagecoach that was effectively in charge of the East Coast operation, with a 90 per cent holding; it had been decided that Virgin's name would appear on the trains, being the stronger brand. History repeats itself somewhat as 43299 bears the name 'LNER' on an up Virgin-liveried train, while the governmental 'operator of last resort' has once again stepped in to run the show. Closer inspection of the power car's cab reveals that the aerial for NRN has long gone from above the windscreen and underneath the wiper can be seen a small camera inside to record a continuous video of the route ahead, in case of incident. The location is Potters Bar and the date 29 October 2018.

LEFT HST sets have been passing regularly through Newcastle since 1977 and continue to do so in 2021. On Saturday, 6 June 1981, a very clean one is seen curving towards the High Level Bridge with a less than usual working, the 13.10 to Scarborough (via York). One can imagine hearing the characteristic sighing from the air suspension of its mark 3 coaches as they pass over the intricate pointwork and diamond crossovers at the north end of the station. For students of railway track forty years ago, this location was a positive delight with its multitude of crossovers, single and double slips and the odd trap point for good measure. To the left of the station passed several goods lines, while parked in the station itself would always be at least one class 03 shunter with its match truck. A Cravens DMU sits gently ticking over in one of the bay platforms to complete the picture. *Transport Treasury Archive*

RIGHT Onward to 24 April 2010 and it's a very different scene. No. 43251 leads a nine-car set northwards from a slimmed down but busier city station: the Tyne and Wear Metro has made redundant most of the bay platforms to the right side and the resultant space given over to car parking. The goods lines and sidings have been all but abolished, with new platforms constructed either side of the outer station wall, and the famous crossovers have been reduced in scope to just the three double slip diamonds. And, of course, we have the overhead wires in place, the arrival of which would have given impetus to much of the track simplification. Parcels traffic has gone from big stations like this, so no shunting locos or parcels stock are to be seen parked around. Finally, the local DMU of the day is now the dreaded 'Pacer'. *Bob Avery*

Down onto the station platform itself, we have 43251 again but going the other way as a member of East Coast on-board staff waits patiently with her overnight case in tow on 13 March 2010. The vantage point for the previous two photos may be noted above the first coach – the Castle Keep of Newcastle Castle! On the front of this power car, the series of fixing holes around the front nose panel have all been filled, removing dirt traps and making for a much tidier appearance.

Two people in the cab of a train is unusual nowadays and my suspicion here is that the driver is receiving some instruction from an older colleague. The windscreen has been given a brief wash as this train (believed to be 1V39 06.32 Dundee–Plymouth) departs Newcastle's platform 4 mid-morning for the South West on 24 January 2011, with 43303 at the head. I spotted 'Toon' legend Alan Shearer getting on a London train here on one occasion; seeing my camera, he looked a little surprised when I didn't point it at him. Sorry, Alan …

HST – The Train That Saved Britain's Railways

This is York

On the quiet Sunday morning of 18 March 1990 under the grand curved station roof at York, we find 43036 at the rear of a Western Region set forming the 10.38 to Cardiff, when direct services to South Wales were still regarded as a fundamental part of the NE–SW axis; for some reason, they fell out of favour as we moved into the privatised era and no operator has sought to restore them yet. Thankfully, the overhead wires were not allowed to be too intrusive, though the wide gap between platforms 3 and 5 makes it obvious that two more tracks used to pass through here. Penny pinching dictated that not even one should be required in future, however useful that might prove in day-to-day operations. On many occasions I have witnessed freight trains passing through these platforms while frustrated passengers watched the delay minutes for their own train mount up.

RIGHT At the south end of the station, 43068 was at the head of the 10.25 Newcastle to King's Cross and it may well be that HSTs were running in place of electric sets on this particular Sunday. This power car was one of the eight that were fitted with buffers by BR to assist with the phased introduction of class 91s onto the ECML. Curiously, these have never been removed since, which would suggest that the modification was so substantial that nothing has justified the trouble or expense of reversing it. Occasionally the buffer fitment has proved useful and for a time six of them came together to work for Grand Central, but it will be interesting to see whether the preservationists will be keen enough to keep one!

LEFT Feet up on the desk, the driver of 43310 takes a moment to relax during his train's long journey to the north on 22 September 2012. Clearly apparent is the modification to the driver's door that was carried out following the fitment of air conditioning to HST cabs; ECML, Cross Country and Grand Central power cars received a two-section window arrangement whereas others got a less obtrusive vent, both intended for use in the event of air con failure. Since 43110 was re-engined with a considerably less smoky MTU unit (and had '200' added to its number), the roof cowling designed to reduce exhaust staining has also gone and the power car's cleaner outline consequently restored. Note also the trackside telephone; rather like household 'landlines', these are slowly becoming obsolete on the network as every cab now is fitted with GSMR and the act of footplate staff going trackside to make a call is increasingly frowned upon from a safety point of view.

Just a few paces along the platform from the previous shot, the very next frame catches an HST set approaching the station from the north. And we've found a solitary diamond crossover, the only one remaining in the York area (if my Quail Track Maps Eastern edition is to be believed). It is interesting to observe the cleanliness of the ballast in busy station areas nowadays, compared to how it looked thirty to forty years ago and beyond. Steam traction was lubricated with oil on the 'total loss' principle, namely that it would all end up on the track at some point, and diesels proved little better for a long time. Fresh ballast would soon be blackened from the oil that dripped from pipes, joints and exhausts. Electric traction is somewhat cleaner anyway but contemporary manufacturing techniques also mean that diesel engines don't leak lubricant like they used to.

Perhaps the most important junction at York lies 4½ miles to the south of the city: Colton Junction was created in 1983 after the building of the so-called 'Selby Diversion' line, established to avoid possible future subsidence problems under the original route between Selby and Chaloner's Whin Junction resulting from the expansion of the Selby coalfield. The latter was expected to produce huge quantities of coal over several decades but in the event did not live up to expectations, with production ending early in the twenty-first century. The National Coal Board had paid for the construction of the diversion and this proved to be the railway's gain as the latter got a new high-speed stretch of line in place of one that had little potential for improvement. On 2 August 2014, 43274 is seen hurrying off the diversion and over the 125mph junction, the first of its kind to be installed in Britain. The footbridge from which the photograph was taken affords a clear view of how this complicated set of switches operates whenever a new route is set from York Control. To the right of the train can be seen the empty trackbed that was vacated when two of the original four tracks out of York were slued sideways to meet the new route, providing the smoothest curve possible for ECML traffic running at full line speed.

In the Picture

Our second interlude surveys HSTs in all kinds of weather and lighting conditions, together with a look at the last services which brought them regularly into the capital city of London.

Blooming Britain

With images like this, do we need any excuse to look at an HST running through our wonderful British countryside? One plant that has grown to the fore during the lifetime of the train is oilseed rape; this flowering crop has brought great swathes of yellowness to the fields each springtime, the by-product of which has actually been used in trains as bio-fuel. The windows of this Cross Country HST led by 43303 reflect the light from its surroundings, the location being Elford and the train 1S51 Plymouth–Edinburgh, an Arriva Cross Country service. No. 43285 is at the rear. It is slightly ironic that, after being one of the first routes to replace its HSTs with new rolling stock, the Cross Country franchise now appears to be the last to retain them in full-length form! 12 May 2012. *Ben Wheeler*

IN THE PICTURE – BLOOMING BRITAIN

The Wylye Valley between Salisbury and Westbury has presented the railway photographer with an abundance of good locations. Despite the ever-present problem of uncontrolled lineside vegetation, this is still a good area and the relatively peaceful countryside hereabouts often means that you can hear a train coming for a while before it appears. On 30 July 2020, the NMT features 43014 *The Railway Observer* (and 43013 *Mark Carne* on the tail) at Sherrington and works 1Q23 05.56 Reading–Salisbury, during which it went to Exeter and back on the West of England line. In the windows of 975984 (coach 40000 from the original prototype HST) is displayed the following message: 'This train's not on a journey, it's on a mission. This train works 24/7 to keep the railway safe.' More details can be found at web address networkrail.co.uk/nmt.

We have another short HST, although this time it's carrying passengers in Scotland. England's loss is Scotland's gain in many people's eyes as these proven trains, with power plants that are good for many more years, find another service life. No. 43141 (with 43031 on the rear) has just crossed the Allan Water on the approach to Blackford on 8 August 2020 with the 1039 from Queen Street to Aberdeen. Apart from the obvious rosebay willowherb (again!), there is a pleasing array of shades of green in this image, as well as yellows and browns leading to the darker and higher ground beyond: Looking above the front power car, the plateau mountain that can be seen on the left is Stuc a'Chroin and the more conical peak is Ben Vorlich. *Ian Lothian*

IN THE PICTURE – BLOOMING BRITAIN

Autumn can provide some colour too and on this occasion trackside growth seems to be assisting the photographic endeavour, rather than hindering it. No. 43285 clears Tapton Junction and nears Chesterfield station on 20 November 2009 at the front of a service to the South West. When Arriva's cross-country operation reintroduced the HST in May 2008, they seemed to make full use of the ten power cars and five trainsets at their disposal in order to reduce overcrowding. Disappointingly, they chose to cut this back to using just two sets per day for much of the time and commuters in the Bristol, Birmingham and Leeds areas often continued to stand for many of their journeys as a result.

Frozen Sets

I wonder if railway modellers ever try to recreate a train like this. This picture of a snow-encrusted W43182 at Bristol Parkway on 8 January 1985 (operating from Plymouth to Newcastle) illustrates how snow can cause problems for a train, even when it doesn't physically block its path. Whatever has been kicked up by the train can end up as ice around the air intakes on the roof of the trailing power car, potentially inhibiting the engine's performance. Powdery snow was found to penetrate the traction motors and this was addressed by the fitting of a snow shield. With the best of intentions, sometimes problems only come to light after a number of years in service. The driver of this working would probably have made sure the cab droplights of this trailing power car were firmly shut before he left Plymouth. *Arthur Turner/Transport Treasury*

IN THE PICTURE – FROZEN SETS

The West Country is known for its mild climate but when the snow falls it can be as disruptive to transport here as anywhere else in the land. Another cross-country set (with 43191 at its head) is shown but this time at Exeter St David's and heading west. In these conditions, drivers soon find out out whether their windscreen wiper blade is in a serviceable state. It wouldn't matter how heavily the snow fell though as their route knowledge would inform him where all the signals are as well as the line speed limits. Even so, it still takes some nerve to be the one at the front. Note the solitary first-class coach in this seven-coach set, catering for the different kind of clientele anticipated on a corridor that saw more leisure travel than those routes to and from London. *Transport Treasury Archive*

A train kicking up the snow always gives a fair impression of speed, although this one wasn't going all that fast as I'm sure there must be a 70mph restriction around Crofton Curve (on the Berks and Hants route). Decent falls of snow in Wiltshire were quite a rare event, I discovered during the six years that I lived in the area. Persuading my boss to allow me a day's leave at relatively short notice, when I could see that sunshine was likely to follow the fall, was key to this little adventure. I'd been hoping for something a bit more interesting on the day, apart from a procession of HSTs, but who would complain now? An unidentified named power car is trailing the 06.35 from Plymouth to Paddington on 8 February 1996 as it speeds past my car towards the Kennet and Avon Canal.

The 7.30 Edinburgh Waverley–London King's Cross whistles past the crossing box at Grove Road on 27 February 2018; 43318 is the power car closest to the camera. The Great Northern Railway box here was closed in 1998 but curiously retained for use in emergencies. It sits at one of five level crossings that are controlled (via camera) from Ranskill box. It can surely only be a matter of time before these crossings are closed and the roads are re-routed from what is, after all, a principal high-speed railway. *Dafydd Whyles*

Into the Light

IN THE PICTURE – INTO THE LIGHT

LEFT The clean outline of the entire formation of an HST has always made it a very attractive subject for 'glint' lighting. But the evening (or early morning) sun has to be at just the right angle and the quality of its light needs to be there too – the last part I cannot easily define, as it isn't necessarily the brightest sort. How many times have I stood by a railway line in gorgeous lighting only for rail traffic to enter a frustrating lull? Here is one occasion when things came together, helped somewhat by the fact that I knew the location would offer such a possibility and it was also only about a twenty-minute drive from my home. On the evening of Saturday, 21 October 1995, several up HSTs passed Shrivenham. Signal checked by the one preceding it, the speed of this example was somewhat reduced, but at 17.30, 43177 and 43179 are now accelerating on the 16.18 Weston-super-Mare to Paddington. The whole train has caught the setting sun (as has one rail of the down line) but most of all, the clean power car has almost taken on a gold-plated appearance. I mostly used Fujichrome Provia 100 slide film at the time.

ABOVE Newport station is the location for this chilly view of a First Great Western train paused en route to London on 30 December 2000. The open droplight window of the first coach illustrates one aspect of the HST that was rather outdated, even at the time of its introduction. Foreign railway professionals would express their surprise that passengers were expected to open a window and reach out to use the handle to open the door. It also led to a loss of warmth inside the vestibule on days like this as few detraining passengers would bother to close the window after them; not their problem! In later years, travellers more used to automatic doors would often stand and stare as they waited for the door to open, wondering why nothing was happening.

ABOVE The photographer responsible for this image is a member of the Phoenix Railway Circle, a group of enthusiastic railway photographers with an eye for something different. This shot was taken during diversions off the ECML and shows 43277 at Gainsborough Trent Junction being 'given the feather' for the Doncaster direction on 18 November 2018. I'm not exactly sure how this fits in with the oft-quoted 'rule of thirds' but it works well enough for me! *Dafydd Whyles*

RIGHT Powering through the Thames Valley comes 43040 *Bristol St Philip's Marsh* in the late afternoon of 29 November 2014, near Cholsey. In this light, the 'shark's fin' antenna for the train's GSM-R system is very obvious on the roof of the power car (above the van). Despite being retained by Great Western for use in the West Country in its 'Castle' fleet of shortened sets, this power car has become *Berry Pomeroy Castle*; it seems a pity not to have retained a name with such a strong association with the franchise and the train in general.

IN THE PICTURE – INTO THE LIGHT

This is Sonning Cutting at 06.36 on 24 June 2016. We are looking back towards London from the A4 overbridge as 43177 approaches Reading on 3A06, the 06.14 Paddington–Didcot Parkway ECS movement of diagram IW012. Having probably run at line speed for 30-odd miles, the train is now braking hard and the brake dust thrown up can easily be seen in the early morning rays of sunlight that penetrate the cutting. At this date, the scene had yet to be spoilt by the paraphernalia of electrification.

IN THE PICTURE – INTO THE LIGHT

On its first revenue-earning run, the nine-car 'Midland Pullman'-liveried HST set belonging to Locomotive Services Ltd is seen returning to London at East Goscote in Leicestershire on 12 December 2020. The reporting code was 1Z44 out from St Pancras International and 1Z45 back from Crewe; 43055 is the leading power car and 43046 trailing. The 'Nanking Blue' colour took its name from the Chinese porcelain that was a popular import to this country in the eighteenth and nineteenth centuries. A fair amount of modification has been undertaken at the front end – it was certainly not just a case of a repaint: the inner pair of tail lights have been removed and a roof headlight added, presumably to satisfy the latest regulations when no yellow warning area is applied. The horn grille has been renewed too but it's a pity that some of those cantrail grilles couldn't have been straightened; perhaps this was a job that had to be foregone in order to meet a deadline. *Steve Donald*

Shots in the Dark

How very different this railway station is today! St Pancras escaped closure and demolition in the early 1970s and by the late '80s was definitely turning a corner, in terms of passenger numbers. On 4 February 1987, I had finished work for the day (in Hendon) and took my camera and tripod on the train into London to try and catch some 'Peaks', as they were in their last full year of main-line operations. My photographic activities concentrated on the four locomotives that I found there but I must have felt obliged to also record this HST set, as it was taking on its complement of passengers for an evening departure. Time exposure (on Kodachrome 64 film) was forty-five seconds, which is why the minute hand on the station clock is blurred! The power car's engine appears to be ticking over; in the early days of operation, engines would often be completely shut down and the set joined to an electrical shore supply to power the auxiliaries. Turnaround times got reduced as the trains saw more intensive use so it became rare to see that facility being used. Little did I suspect that 43062 would one day feature very strongly in my working life, after it had become one of the three power cars hired by Network Rail for use with the New Measurement Train.

RIGHT Seeing two HST sets together beneath the main overall roof at Bristol Temple Meads became something of a rarity in later years, as London services tended to start and finish from the island platform on the east side of the station. However, the time of day may have had something to do with it here, as it was 04.20 on the morning of Saturday, 23 November 1991. Again, I'm there out of interest for something else, being a participant on Pathfinder Tours' 'Valiant Thunderer' trip to Newquay with class 50s featuring strongly. Shamefully I have omitted to record the identities of these power cars, though my excuse would be the more pressing need to be at the other end of the station in preparedness for the appearance of 50008 *Thunderer* and 50015 *Valiant* at the head of the railtour. Note the brightly lit double-sided St Andrew's Cross indicator, demarking the boundary between platforms 5 and 6.

LEFT It is now 6 February 2003 and again I'm minded to spend a few hours of an evening after work with my tripod at my nearest large station. This time it's Nottingham and once again, I'm here for a different purpose, namely to see the passage of the Structure Gauging Train, which I knew would be stopping en route to a night's monitoring on the Skegness line. No. 43077 has just arrived at the rear of a service from St Pancras and the driver seems to have kindly left the cab light on, although somehow I doubt it was for my benefit. I commuted through Nottingham for a time in the late 1990s and recall one winter's evening when the station suffered a complete power failure just before the rush hour. In near darkness, a confident member of station staff stood at the top of the footbridge stairs with a loud hailer, announcing train departures to the anxious throng below.

The staff at Etches Park depot referred to the fuelling shed there as the 'Wind Tunnel', due to its orientation seemingly being just right for the prevailing wind to blow straight through it, especially in winter. So fuelling trains on a night like this was never going to be one of their more pleasant tasks. Late in the evening of 16 February 2007, the exhaust from 43014 billows up into the roof while being attended to, after working from Old Oak Common to Swansea earlier that day and then back to Derby. Although convenient for its proximity to the Railway Technical Centre, full maintenance of the NMT had been moved away from Etches Park some time before, following difficulties that Maintrain were having in servicing Midland Mainline's own fleet of HSTs.

IN THE PICTURE – SHOTS IN THE DARK

No. 43037 waits in platform 5 at Temple Meads before departing with the 17.30 to Paddington on 19 December 2008. This power car had been named *Penydarren Rail Bicentenary 1804-2004* at Cardiff in 2004 to mark the 200th anniversary of the running of Trevithick's steam locomotive, heading the world's first proper train. On refurbishment (with a new MTU power unit) in 2007, the nameplates were removed from 43037 but they did seem to find their way back onto the power car at some point. Now that it is working for Scotrail, the plates have been removed again, which I think is regrettable. If a name is deemed worthy of application in the first place, it deserves to remain there until the locomotive completes its service.

Here is a scene that must have been played out many times over the years. We are looking into the covered stabling roads at Old Oak Common at 04.50 on 28 October 2011, a weekday, as several cleaned, watered and fuelled HST sets wait to proceed to Paddington to begin their day's service. From left we have 43137 *Newton Abbot 150*, 43168, one unidentified and 43022 plus a class 57 further back on 15 road. No. 43137 has a driver in the cab and is clearly about to move off. Arriving at the depot just after 04.00, I had carried out my own preparation duties on the NMT parked nearby and with a few minutes to spare before our own departure to Plymouth, took the opportunity to record this view using a five-second exposure. Depots such as Old Oak were specially configured to address the issues of having to service dirtier power cars alongside cleaner coaches.

RIGHT It's a green for the up main. The long reign of the HST on the ECML was drawing to a close on 30 December 2018 as 43320 paused at the south end of York station's platform 3, ready for a fast run down to 'The Cross'. As ever, there are no shortage of reminders in place about where trains should stop – I'm sure the sign producers have been kept happy. I was under the impression that drivers would habitually pull up to a platform end signal anyway in case they needed to use the SPT (signal post telephone), thus saving themselves too long a walk. And to me, that 'N' in LNER looks suspiciously like part of an upturned BR double-arrow! It is believed the power cars that spent their entire service lives working on the ECML (up to 2019) had completed around 10 million miles each.

BELOW The headlights of 43081 stab at the fog as it swirls around platform 1 at Derby station on 23 January 2017. This was 1F70, the 19.55 London St Pancras International to Leeds service, and 43059 brought up the rear. This late-evening trip was diagrammed to end at Leeds, rather than the usual Sheffield, as the set would end up at Neville Hill depot that night anyway. It's at times like these that you get to properly appreciate the safety and comfort of rail travel; not many people would relish having to drive 100 miles or so home on an evening like this, no matter what sort of road vehicle they had. And I would include an autonomous one!
Steve Donald

Closing Credits

With just a few weeks to go before EMR declared they would end the use of HSTs, I sought to capture some of their workhorses from some different angles as they carried out the final regular duties of an HST, into and out of the capital city. April 2021 was largely fine, often sunny and unseasonably dry in the south of England so there were few excuses for staying at home! Crossing the Bedford southern by-pass, this working on the 22nd was 1D43, the 14.34 St Pancras International–Nottingham, and 43274 is in the lead. I've always felt that the sight of an express shooting over a bridge above a busy main road acts as a reminder to motorists that, for long-distance travel, the train cannot be beaten; you may drive the most potent vehicle money can buy but the speed limit is still 70 and for an HST that's dawdling.

IN THE PICTURE – CLOSING CREDITS

East Midland Railway's 43238 was referred to as the 'Flying Tomato', thanks to its all-over base red livery that remained from previous service on Virgin East Coast and LNER. As the final power car to receive a major 'exam' at Edinburgh's Craigentinny depot, the MTU power unit itself was said to have been sprayed with gold paint to mark the occasion! At 110mph, a shutter speed of 1/2,000 second barely freezes the action as 1D48 15.34 St Pancras International–Nottingham storms up to Sharnbrook under a clear blue sky (one hour after the previous image). The small Ferrari sticker on the nose hatch of 43238 caught many people's attention!

IN THE PICTURE – CLOSING CREDITS

LEFT This arch in the road bridge at Harlington station was something that caught my eye as a photographic possibility. This is the shadow side of the train but being so head on to the camera, that is less important; the difference is that the inside of the arch is that much darker, helping the colour on the front of the train to stand out even more. Alternative photographic judgments are available! On 23 April 2021, 43309 (and 43272) are on route refresher duty with this 5M17 10.20 departure from St Pancras International, out via Corby and back via Leicester.

ABOVE A closer look at 43274 under the St Pancras 'extension' roof on 26 April 2021. To mark the ending of HST working on the Midland, EMR chose to apply their new house colours to 43274, something that led many to remark that it was a pity a complete set would never be turned out in a similar fashion. A few problems were experienced in the final weeks when over-enthusiastic passengers leaned out of the window excessively during running, much to the concern of the operating staff. *John Tidmarsh*

Out of the Ordinary

Diversions, specials and breakdowns; they've been many and varied in the life of the High Speed Train. These are just a flavour of them.

Diversionary Tactics

No. 43179 *Pride of Laira* takes the diverted 09.35 Paddington–Paignton service over the Melksham line at Broughton Gifford on 12 March 1994. This very useful 8-mile long piece of single line runs from Thingley Junction (outside Chippenham) to Bradford Junction in Wiltshire. Normally it supports a sparse passenger service that serves the small town of Melksham, the station having been closed between 1966 and 1985 and at other times, down to two trains each way per day. It has probably owed its survival in the past to freight traffic, with private sidings serving various facilities in Melksham (now all closed) and aggregates coming from the Mendip quarries. However, it also regularly earns its keep as a diversionary route for trains off the Berks & Hants or from the Bristol and South Wales route. At the invitation of Plymouth Area Fleet Manager Geoff Hudson, a member of the depot's admin staff, Glynis Deighton, named 43179 at the Laira depot open day on 15 September 1991. Hopefully one more such event may be staged there before its long association with HSTs finally comes to an end.

One further most useful link for diversions has to be the East Loop at Westbury. No doubt it was considered for closure during the Westbury area resignalling in 1985 but sensibly has been retained. Although freight services do make use of it, it comes into its own for diversions between the respective main routes to the west by reducing the need for time-consuming reversals in Westbury station itself. This is the Hawkeridge Junction end of the loop at 15.15 on 26 June 2005, as 43183 brings up the rear of a Paddington-bound train that was headed by 43031. Being less than half a mile long, this sharp curve could accommodate an HST within its signalling section but longer freight consists would overhang at one end. That 'SW' warning board is a bit of a survivor, and note the two sections of rail in the four foot of the opposite track being used to strap the four sleepers together around a rail adjustment switch (special joints to allow rail expansion).

Still operational at the time of writing is the crossing box at Swinderby in Lincolnshire. Being so low and small, this Midland Railway Type 3a design from 1901 might justifiably be called a 'cabin' rather than a box. What is unusual about this crossing is that, due to its skewed nature, only the one gate shown here can be swung across the railway when it is open for road traffic; the other is set too far back from the line to serve that purpose. During weekend diversion working from the ECML, we see 43108 fronting an Aberdeen to King's Cross train (with 43116 *City of Kingston upon Hull* for company) on 24 May 1998. Electric sets were using class 47s to see them over the diversion ('dragged', in enthusiast parlance) between Newark Northgate and Doncaster.

Approaching Donington (between Sleaford and Spalding) on 16 October 2010, 43313 helps to make up an immaculate set of vehicles working the diverted 1E10 07:52 Aberdeen–London King's Cross East Coast service. This planned diversion via the GN/GE Joint Line was because of engineering work between Newark and Peterborough; 43257 was bringing up the rear. Just as the power stations mentioned elsewhere vanish from our landscape, so a new form of power generation has begun to take their place. Wind turbines may not be well received everywhere they are built but they have become a familiar fixture in the twenty-first century. *Ben Wheeler*

Sweeping round the curves near Low Row on the crucial Newcastle–Carlisle line goes a diverted GNER HST. This is another normally relatively quiet railway that earns its keep on the network whenever the main ECML link over the border gets blocked. The arrangement rarely works in reverse as WCML traffic has the option of travelling via Dumfries. GNER started applying names to power cars with gold stick-on lettering but 43300 *Craigentinny* re-acquired its old name with a proper nameplate (perhaps the depot staff insisted on that) – together with the new number (from 43100). No. 43300 had been the first of this fleet to receive the MTU power unit in the previous November, coupled with further more extensive improvements similar to those given to previously re-engined power cars with FGW. GNER was struggling to fulfil the premium payments in its franchise agreement at this time and the bodyside adverts were perhaps a clear indication of their problems. 6 October 2007. *Keith Sanders*

OUT OF THE ORDINARY – DIVERSIONARY TACTICS

RIGHT Over the Easter holiday weekend of 2013, a partial closure of Reading station entailed the diversion of HSTs that normally ran through Swindon, to go via a reversal at Banbury, en route to Paddington; West Country services used Waterloo. With a conductor sat in the secondman's old seat, 43032 sweeps through Princes Risborough on the through line on 31 March. The magnificent North signalbox here was in dire need of attention at the time, access for Chinnor Railway volunteers having been denied by Network Rail for several years. However, NR Route Director Dyan Crowther knocked some heads together and the structure was saved in the nick of time; it is now in much better shape and watches over the preserved railway's restored service into a new platform 4. Two through lines used to grace this station but short-term decision-making has made it difficult to put back more than one, it would seem.

LEFT 43163 makes a Sunday diversion via Avonmouth on 19 February 1984 whilst working from Leeds to Plymouth (accompanied by 43190). Hallen Marsh Junction still had its ex-Great Western signalbox and a fine array of lower quadrant signalling at the time, though all would be gone come 1988. The chemical industry seems to be busy enough here, and the duty signalman probably had all kinds of odours to put up with, should the wind ever blow in the wrong direction! *Arthur Turner/Transport Treasury*

Trouble

One of the undoubted strengths of the High Speed Train over the years has been the provision of 'head end' power at both ends of the train. The Blue Pullman of the 1960s began the trend in that regard, but the ability to change a set's direction in a matter of minutes and to continue running, should one of the power cars fail, proved of enormous benefit. However, that clearly hasn't happened on this occasion: 43023 sits in the centre siding at Worcester Shrub Hill on a quiet Sunday morning on 17 July 1988, presumably having been removed from a train following severe problems with its running gear. Twelve years after introduction, this power car still proclaims its original set number of 253011, long after the inevitable exchanging of power cars had rendered such detail irrelevant. The process of 'Sprinterisation' was in full swing at the time; we can see two class 155 DMUs calling at the station with up and down services linking Birmingham and Cardiff.

Yellow and black livery, anyone? Power car 43014 sits shamefacedly outside Etches Park depot in Derby on 16 September 2003. On being required to power the New Measurement Train alone for many miles, when its travelling partner had given up the ghost at an earlier stage, it too cried 'enough' and blew its turbocharger. The engine 'spat its dummy out', as one of my former colleagues might have put it, although what has come out and all down its flank is a lot of engine oil. The three power cars taken on by NR to work the NMT weren't in the best of health at first and several failures in service were the result. Nobody was really surprised, I recall, as the train was somewhat late into service and there wasn't time to put them through a proper programme of overhaul; that would come later and reliability (thankfully) improved no end.

I was working in air transport and living in Swindon at the time I took this photo, on 19 July 1993. Somebody from the office, having driven through Wootton Bassett, rang me to say that there'd been a train crash near the old station. Nothing had been reported on the radio or television but I hurried over there to find this state of affairs: 43175 and 43163 had been sandwiching coach 41167 on an ECS move from St Philip's Marsh to Old Oak, only for things to go a little awry in the goods loop. At a guess I would say that on arriving at the signal here, the driver had left his cab to call the box, only to see his train move forward without him. Or possibly there has been some sort of brake malfunction with this irregular formation. The trap point has done its work and protected the main line from the runaway. It's a warm summer's evening, so every man and his dog has apparently put on an orange vest and turned out to 'help'. The fire engine was probably called out in case of a fuel leak and is about to depart the scene. A late-running train approaches from the Bath direction at reduced speed, passengers leaning from every door window to see what the fuss is about. It was one of those mishaps that reminded me of a Thomas the Tank engine story featuring a sad-faced engine in the dirt, feeling sorry for itself and wondering what the Fat Controller would have to say.

ABOVE Near Arlesey on the ECML, we see a particularly rare sight heading northwards on 23 October 2007. No. 91130 *City of Newcastle* is dragging 43051 at the head of a failed set that had been forming 1S22 15.30 King's Cross–Edinburgh. Thunderbird locomotives on the ECML tended to be class 67 diesels hired from EWS but an electric loco was clearly spare for the duty at the time, keeping the work 'in house', as it were. Driver Manager Mick Barstow said that he had conducted an assessment on the Thunderbird driver earlier in the day: The 91 was coupled up using the HST's emergency coupler plus an adaptor 'wedge' carried on all class 91s, in case of this infrequent event. Lucky Mick still had time to travel home and be in position to take the photograph! *Mick Barstow*

RIGHT This shows why buffers were fitted to some of the East Coast power cars chosen to work as DVTs: The unique Brush-designed Co-Co electric locomotive, number 89001 is shown leading one of them out of Leeds station with an up express to London on 19 November 1988. It was said that the design of this loco was influenced by the HST and its body profile took after that of the mark 3 coach. Sadly, no sooner had it emerged from BREL's Crewe Works than BR decided to go for fixed formation trains on the electrified ECML with an intended top speed of 140mph; the class 89 was only capable of 125mph and its freight-hauling capability would not be required. It may yet be seen again on the main line. *Arthur Turner/Transport Treasury*

Special Workings

The 31 August 1975 witnessed a grand cavalcade of trains in the North East at the end of a week marking the 150th anniversary of the opening of the Stockton and Darlington Railway. On what is clearly a warm day at Shildon, the prototype set 252001 (which had entered regular service on 5 May that year) rolls past many onlookers, who may well have been wondering whether this really was the future of our railways. Well, I think we can now confirm that it was indeed! During the early 1970s, the HST and APT projects appeared to be proceeding almost neck and neck at times, with both prototypes undergoing test runs at full speed on the main line. The HST was given the green light to go into full production, however, whilst the APT became bogged down with a variety of issues that saw any entry into regular service being repeatedly put back. Initially given the locomotive numbers 41001 and 41002, the protoype's power cars were aligned with the class 43 production power cars and numbered W43000 and W43001, before entering the departmental fleet as RDB975812/3 in late 1976. *John Tolson/Transport Treasury*

OUT OF THE ORDINARY – SPECIAL WORKINGS

Movements of redundant or re-employed HST power cars (and rolling stock generally) became a regular sight as they were retired by the longer-distance operators. And with the help of online information sources, hardly any of this went unnoticed, in contrast to earlier times when it was often a chance encounter that led to unusual workings being photographed. The deep blue paintwork of the power cars seen here is beginning to look decidedly faded, having been parked up for a year or so, nameplates removed. On 15 September 2020, 43029 and 43027 are paired up for this assault on the Lickey Incline, while on their way from Laira to Doncaster Works, reporting code 5Z23. Also in this formation was 43022 (formerly *The Duke of Edinburgh's Award Diamond Anniversary 1956-2016*), mark 3s 42087 and 42580 plus Rail Operations Group's 47815 *Lost Boys 68-88* with its barrier mark 1 6340. The farmyard detritus may hint at some of these rail vehicles being put out to grass but is it too early to suggest that the wheels have come off their railway career for good? *Dave Besley*

In contrast to Dawlish, at Blue Anchor on the West Somerset Railway there is no hefty sea wall to separate a stormy sea from the trains. However, the waves rarely threaten here in the way that they do in South Devon. On 23 September 2017, 43042 led the 'Cotswold–Quantock Explorer' from Oxford to Minehead, with 43154 in the supporting role. The train had run out via a reversal at Worcester Shrub Hill and returned there later in the evening, via Didcot West Curve and Oxford. The wide route availability of the power cars and coaches permitted all kinds of branch line excursions to be undertaken by HSTs. It was John Farrow of Hertfordshire Railtours who first took advantage of this in 1988, when he persuaded BR to utilise a spare MML set for these tours at weekends. Very popular they were too! *Kelvin Lumb*

Locomotive Services Ltd's 'Midland Pullman' set consists of power cars 43055 and 43046 *Geoff Drury 1930-1999*, together with vehicles 41176, 41108, 40802, 41162, 41059, 41182, 40801, 41169 and 44078. These numbers are preceded by an 'M' as a nod to the original 'Midland Pullman' train. On a sunny day such as this one, the livery stands out superbly and can only have grabbed the attention of anyone who happened to witness its progress. Having operated the 'Cornish Coastal Pullman' from Eastleigh to Penzance the previous day, it is shown passing the buttercups of a very wet meadow at King's Sutton on the following Sunday afternoon of 30 May 2021, going back to Crewe as 5Z64 12.54 Eastleigh Arlington–Crewe Holding Sidings. The spire of St Peter & St Paul church provides the very English backdrop to this scene. All being well, I shall have ridden this train to Devon by the time this book has been published.

Ever Onward...

It's not all over yet and HSTs will continue to be seen in many parts of the country for some time to come. How many locomotives or trains from the past have been around long enough to celebrate 50 years in front line service? 2026 is not so far off...

A brief reuse of power cars on Network Rail test trains, apart from the New Measurement Train, came about in the autumn of 2020; though at the time of writing this development had yet to be pursued any further. In place of aged class 37 locomotives, former EMT power cars 43060 and 43050 carry Colas Rail symbols as they sandwich a PLPR formation of four vehicles near Bruerne on the Cotswold route – 43060 appears on the front of this book in its previous role. 1Z22 was the 08.20 Tyseley to Bristol High Level Siding (via Didcot, Weymouth and Hallen Marsh Junction!) on 4 November 2020 and would be using object recognition software to flag up missing or damaged track components, as well as any deficiencies in track alignment. Other former EMT power cars, together with class 91s redundant from the ECML, have seen use on electrification proving specials over the MML north of Bedford.

RIGHT The launch of Rail Charter Services Ltd's 'Staycation Express' over the Settle and Carlisle route in late July 2021 demanded a trip to this ever popular part of North Yorkshire. As it happened, the response to the question often asked of anyone stood beside a railway with a camera: 'Is The Flying Scotsman coming?' would have been 'Yes', for once. However, 'Flying Scotsman' (without the 'the'!) had passed northwards earlier on Saturday 24 July and was not the most important attraction for me anyway. A move, from a cloudy vantage point near Blea Moor, to Ais Gill was rewarded with sunshine at the critical moment as 43059 led coaches 41187, 40804, 41160, 41166 and 44081 plus 43058 on 1Z44, the 15.09 from Carlisle to Skipton. Could additional HST sets find even further use on charter trains across Britain, if an effort to find extra pathing was made?

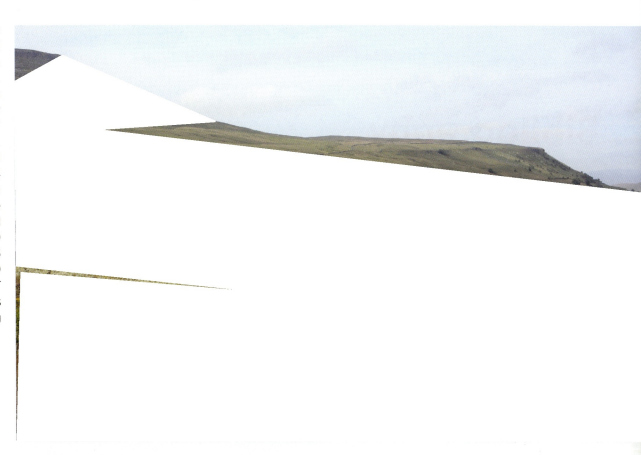

LEFT To encourage rail passengers to abide by the rule to wear a face covering during the pandemic, someone had the bright idea of applying a mock one to the front of a train. Perhaps this was only going to work with a front-end nose so HSTs, Pendolinos and Azumas were in the frame for that! No. 43129 has arrived punctually at Glasgow Queen Street on the 08.45 from Inverness on Friday, 21 May 2021. Power car 43145 was also noted with a mask, which surely should have extended across the horn grille to be properly effective! Comment was made in the media that HSTs were being retired as they didn't comply with modern access requirements and discharged toilet waste to the track. Scotrail would appear to hold a different view and we can expect to see them running over non-electrified lines for some while yet.

Bibliography

125 The Enduring Icon, 125 Group: Amberley Publishing 2018

The Blue Pullman Story, Kevin Robertson and Mike Smith: Crécy Publishing 2020.

HST, The Second Millennium, Colin J. Marsden: Ian Allan 2010

The InterCity Story, Chris Green & Mike Vincent: Oxford Publishing 2013

Modern Locomotives Illustrated No. 246: HSTs-The New Era, edited by Colin J. Marsden

Modern Railways magazine

Railway Magazine

Rail Enthusiast magazine

Railway Track Diagrams published by Trackmaps

Yellow Trains: Ten Years of Testing, Andrew Royle: Crécy Publishing 2019

doublearrow.co.uk website

Index

Power Cars

Number	Pages
43000 (41001)	98, 99, 100
43001 (ADB975813)	16
43002	13, 29, 55, 57, 98, 99, 101
43003	28, 78
43004	113
43005	13, 24
43008	23, 25
43009	80, 87
43013	80, 91, 98, 100
43014	105, 115, 124, 134, 149, 164, 179
43016	10
43018	102
43022	31, 102, 166
43023	178
43024	19
43025	50
43026	26
43027	183
43028	18, 60, 85, 110
43029	17, 86, 183
43031	107
43032	177
43036	144
43037	33, 85, 165
43039	65
43040	68, 159
43042	48, 184
43043	8, 64
43044	46, 89
43045	36
43046	84
43047	81, 109
43048	98
43051	66, 127, 181
43053	66
43054	80, 129
43055	161, 185
43058	128
43059	187
43060	cover, 53, 186
43061	83
43062	45, 63, 81, 122, 123, 125, 162
43063	7, 114
43064	64
43066	11, 49
43067	70, 71, 72, 73, 74
43068	117, 145
43069	6, 54
43070	121
43071	108
43072	88
43073	129
43075	16, 126
43077	163
43079	66
43080	136
43081	38, 167
43083	120
43086	32, 80, 116
43087	14, 90, 91, 104
43089	66, 82
43090	92
43091	92
43093	39
43100	43
43102	1, 15
43107	52
43108	174
43112	81
43118	81
43123	43, 79
43124	68
43125	46
43127	47
43128	79
43129	5, 187
43130	42
43131	44
43136	40
43137	166
43138	67
43141	150
43142	21, 38, 119
43143	42
43144	61
43145	30, 67
43150	44
43152	65
43154	87, 105
43158	115
43159	61, 87
43160	118
43163	177
43166	49
43165	15
43168	166
43172	98
43173	9
43175	180
43177	156, 160
43179	12, 27, 172
43180	51, 80
43182	152
43183	22, 173
43185	55
43187	20, 29, 31, 98
43190	35

189

43191 153	**Liveries**	**Locations**
43192 .... 11, 112, 188	BR Original 14, 16, 29, 42, 48,	Abbots Ripton 65
43193 120	51, 70, 86, 92, 93, 99, 101, 102,	Ais Gill 187
43196 .... 85, 90, 91	140, 152, 153, 177, 182	Aller Jn 51, 119
43207 34	BR Executive 5-9, 15, 43, 65,	Arlesey 181
43238 .... 132, 169	71, 162, 163, 178, 181	Aviemore 107
43251 .... 88, 136, 141, 142	BR InterCity 1, 10-13, 17, 19,	Avonmouth 177
43257 .... 44, 138	26, 27, 36, 46, 52, 55-59, 71, 78,	Bath Spa 23
43274 .... 49, 147, 168, 171	79, 85, 103, 144, 145,	Beckfoot 114
43277 .... 16, 58	154, 156, 172, 180	Bedford 168
43285 151	Great Western (Merlin) 20, 22-25	Berwick 130, 132
43295 131	First Great Western 28, 79, 80, 98, 102,	Birmingham New St 65, 87
43299 139	119, 157	Blackford 49, 150
43300 .... 98, 100, 130, 176	First Great Western (Blue) 18, 21, 28,	Blue Anchor 184
43301 37	30-33, 35, 38, 40, 44, 50, 54, 60, 61,	Bristol 13, 24, 67, 79,
43302 106	67-69, 85, 87, 110-113, 159, 160,	163, 165
43303 .... 143, 148	165, 170, 173, 177, 183, 184	Bristol Parkway 5, 123, 152
43306 88	Great Western (Green) 29, 31, 39, 98	Bromsgrove 118, 183
43308 62	Cross Country 35, 37, 41,	Bruerne 186
43309 170	106, 143, 148, 151	Burton on Trent 115
43310 145	Virgin 43, 65, 72, 80,	Carlisle 103
43313 .... 131, 175	87, 114-118	Cheltenham 9
43314 137	Virgin East Coast/LNER 49, 98,	Chesterfield 11, 109, 151
43317 .... 88, 130	100, 106, 130-134, 139,	Chevinside 120, 127
43318 155	155, 158, 167	Cholsey 159
43320 167	GNER 66, 73, 81, 136,	Churchdown 63
43357 41	174, 176, 181	Cockwood Harbour 41
43378 106	Nat Express/East Coast 44, 62, 88, 136-138,	Colton Jn 147
43423 .... 98, 100	141, 142, 145-147, 175	Cossington 75
43467 .... 74, 75, 76	Midland Mainline 38, 46, 49, 53, 64, 66, 90,	Craigentinny 91
43480 .... 77, 139	104, 108, 109, 120,	Crewe 92, 115
43484 83	126, 127, 163	Cricklewood 84, 89
	East Midlands Trains .... cover, 75, 83,	Crofton 18-21, 154
	84, 88, 89, 98, 120,	Dainton Tunnel 22
	128, 129, 167	Darlington 123
	East Midlands Railway 76, 168-171	Dauntsey 56
	Scotrail 47, 107, 135, 150, 187	Dawlish 37-40
	Grand Central 74, 83, 98, 136, 139	Derby 14-16, 73,
	Network Rail 45, 63, 73, 81, 82, 87, 91,	80, 81, 90, 104, 122,
	98, 105, 122-125, 134,	164, 167, 179
	149, 164, 179, 186	Didcot 50, 54, 60
	Cotswold Rail 91, 121	Doncaster 71
	Pullman 161, 185	Donington 175
	Rail Charter Services 187	East Goscote 161
	railadventure 77	Eastleigh 77
		Edinburgh 73, 106
		Elford 148
		Euston 43
		Evesham 121

Exeter	11, 29, 48, 102, 153
Ferme Park	82
Ferrybridge	55
Findhorn Viaduct	135
Forth Bridge	133
Gainsborough	158
Glasgow Queen St	187
Grantham	95, 139
Hadley Wood	6
Harlington	170
Hatfield	70
Heaton	74, 83
High Wycombe	112
Honeybourne	61, 91
Houndwood	130, 136
Inverness	47
Kingham	110
King's Cross	44, 66, 88, 131, 136
King's Sutton	185
Largin Viaduct	31
Lea Marston	100
Leeds	71, 138, 181
Leicester	49, 128
Longsight	85
Lostwithiel	30
Low Row	176
Maidenhead	61
Manchester Piccadilly	108
Melksham	172
Millbrook	76
Neville Hill	17, 81, 83, 88
Newark	62, 155
Newcastle	140-143
Newport	102, 157
Newton Abbot	113
Norton Bridge	12, 116
Nottingham	120, 163
Old Oak Common	85, 166
Paddington	42, 44, 45, 86, 97
Pembroke Dock	29
Penzance	105
Pilning	27, 58
Plymouth	31, 74, 105
Potters Bar	139
Prestonpans	137
Princes Risborough	177
Ratcliffe	53
Rugeley	117
St Pancras	46, 64, 126, 162, 171
St Philip's Marsh	78, 79, 98, 99
Settle Jn	124
Severn Tunnel Jn	28
Sharnbrook	cover, 8, 129, 169
Sheffield	129
Sherrington	149
Shildon	182
Shrivenham	110, 111, 156
Sonning Cutting	68, 160
Stoke on Trent	72
Stratford	16
Swansea	87
Swinderby	174
Swindon	26
Tamar Bridge	33
Taunton	28
Tay Bridge	134
Teignmouth	36
Torquay	32
Totnes	34, 25, 106
Trent Jn	52, 66
Tring	125
Waterloo	46
Wellingborough	7
Westbury	173
Woodborough	57
Wootton Bassett	180
Worcester	13, 25, 178
Yeovil Pen Mill	10
York	101, 144-146, 167

43192 seems to have a lighting problem here and is our tail-end Charlie with a tail-lamp. *Transport Treasury Archive*